Forewo

THE PA†H TO
different

How the Story of Caleb Teaches Us to Live a Life of Purpose and Impact

LONNIE FREE

Cover Design by 100Covers.com
Interior Design by FormattedBooks.com

To Taylor,

You are the embodiment of a difference maker. Your love for Jesus and your desire to serve others is unmatched. It is such a privilege that I get to spend my life with you. I love you!

CONTENTS

FOREWORD

Lonnie is a young man with much passion that's been placed in the right direction. I encourage young men that have a passion to write, to start now instead of later. Lonnie has taken the life of Caleb, which happens to be my favorite Old Testament character, a man that I feel wanted when he was finishing life, what he wanted when he started his walk with all mighty God. Lonnie looks into this man that has a different spirit, simply entitles his book after that thought and then begins to delineate the truth that can be exposed in the life of a person with a different spirit. This generation like past generations, stands in dire need of people with a different spirit. Those that really desire to be different makers. Their hope being that God would greatly use them to impact their generation and the generations that follow up. I believe that every student and every adult that reads and meditates on this truth will be exposed to that which can help you to become a difference maker. Life is short. We are referred to as a hand's breath, just vapor. And in this brief time that we're here, we can be difference makers, making an eternal difference. May that be true of you and of me. Thank you, Lonnie, for taking the life of a man, placing alongside the truth that is exposed and encouraging us to embrace it for our own good and for His glory.

Johnny M. Hunt

Dr. Johnny Hunt
Sr. Pastor First Baptist Church Woodstock
Senior Vice President of Evangelism and Pastoral Leadership,
North American Mission Board

CHAPTER 1

THE DESIRE TO BE A DIFFERENCE MAKER

"Those who follow the crowd usually get lost in it."[1]
Rick Warren, author of *The Purpose Driven Life*

"What is my purpose?" As a youth pastor, I get asked that question all the time. People are longing to live meaningful lives that impact the world around them. We want our lives to count. If we are honest with ourselves, we all want to make a difference. If I were to ask you if you wanted to waste your life, your answer would be an emphatic: "No." But, the fact is, many people are wasting their lives. Why? The answer is simple. Most people are spending all their time and energy into fitting in, instead of trying to make a difference. However, what I've come to realize is that you must be different to make a difference.

That is the whole idea behind this book. We are going to unpack together what it means for your life to be different so that you can live a life of impact for the kingdom of God. Just a heads up, you will not be able to accomplish this out of your own power and will.

This book is meant to be practical, but you can't depend on yourself to live it out. It is intended to push you towards reliance on God to work through you.

In the Bible, we find someone who will be our model of what it looks like to be different. This is not a how-to book that tells you to be like this person because he was flawed just like you and me. However, the Bible says that this person had a "different spirit," and there are some valuable principles that we can learn from his life. His name is Caleb, and here is his story.

Caleb and the Twelve Spies

Caleb was an Israelite. The ancient Israelites were slaves in Egypt until a man named Moses freed them. When Moses led the Israelites away from Egypt, they came to a land that God had promised them. Before they entered the land, however, Moses sent twelve spies into the area for forty days to see what it was like. Caleb was one of these twelve spies. Here is their report:

> *"And they told him, 'We came to the land to which you sent us. It flows with milk and honey, and this is its fruit.'"*
> Numbers 13:27 ESV

In other words, the land was good! It was exactly how God promised them in Exodus 3:8, a land flowing with milk and honey. It was the perfect place for the Israelites to dwell.

> *"'However, the people who dwell in the land are strong, and the cities are fortified and very large. And besides, we saw the descendants of Anak there. The Amalekites dwell in the land of the Negeb. The Hittites, the Jebusites, and the Amorites dwell in the hill country. And the Canaanites dwell by the sea, and along the Jordan.'*

But Caleb quieted the people before Moses and said,
'Let us go up at once and occupy it, for we are well
able to overcome it.' Then the men who had gone
up with him said, 'We are not able to go up against
the people, for they are stronger than we are.'"
Numbers 13:28-31 ESV

The other spies said the land was good, but the people who inhabited the area were too strong, and their cities were also fortified and very large. Caleb came to a different conclusion. God wasn't very pleased with what the other spies had to say, but here is what He had to say about Caleb:

*"But my servant Caleb, **because he has a different spirit***
and has followed me fully, I will bring into the land into
which he went, and his descendants shall possess it."
Numbers 14:24 ESV

What would it look like for someone to have a different spirit now? What is the purpose that drives this kind of person? What kind of impact would that someone have on the world?

Revival for a New Generation

I recently attended a program called Student Leadership University. If you don't know what that is, it is a phenomenal organization that teaches students about leadership from a Christian perspective. The conference was in Orlando, Florida, and we flew there from Birmingham, Alabama. On the plane ride there, I was reading a book called *Jesus Revolution* by Greg Laurie. The book is all about the Jesus movement of the late 60s and early 70s. I was intrigued by the way that God moved in this unlikely generation of hippies and drug addicts. It was not a perfect movement, and it had its shortcomings.

But thousands of people were saved in these years, and many went on to become faithful, lifelong followers of Jesus. After reading this book, I kept thinking about this question: "What would it look like for God to move in this generation?"

Fast forward a few days, and I am sitting in one of the sessions at Student Leadership University. Dr. Jay Strack was speaking, and he asked us, "What would you do for the kingdom of God if you knew you couldn't fail?"

Wow! Now, that is something to pause and think about for a moment. Then, Dr. Jay had us write down our response to that question, and he had us think about what our dream was. I thought about it for a few minutes, and then, it came to me. I wrote that my dream is to be a part of a movement of God in this generation.

I believe that this generation is full of infinite potential and that we can see another great move of God. But, before that happens, an inner movement must take place in the lives of many believers, and we must stop falling into the trap of trying to fit in with the rest of the world. Christians are called to be different. We are not called to fit in but to be difference makers. Caleb's life gives us a valuable insight into how to do this.

I hope these pages impact you, and I believe with all my heart that you are not reading this book right now by accident. Maybe, you will come to have a relationship with Jesus for the first time. Perhaps, you have been a Christian for a while now, but you lack the passion you once had. Maybe, you are already a mature believer, but there are some things God wants to show you through this book. Whatever your situation may be, my prayer is that God will move in your life like never before. I pray that your desire to be a difference-maker merges with God's desire to be glorified in your life.

You will probably recognize areas in your life that you need to make some changes. That's okay, none of us have it all figured out. If you think you do, then you don't know yourself very well. Here's my challenge to you. Own those areas in your life that you need to make changes. Say to yourself, "I need to be different in this area so I can make a difference for the kingdom of God." Don't just read this book. Implement it in your everyday life.

Discussion

1. Describe your desire to make a difference. What impact do you wish to make on the world?

2. Why do you need to be different in order to make a difference?

3. How have you been trying to fit in when God has called you to stand out?

4. What areas do you need to be different in order to make a difference?

CHAPTER 2

A DIFFERENT SPIRIT ENCOURAGES INSTEAD OF DISCOURAGES

"But Caleb quieted the people before Moses and said, 'Let us go up at once and occupy it, for we are well able to overcome it.'"
Numbers 13:30

If you want to have a different spirit and if you're going to make a difference, it is beneficial to think back to the people who have made a difference in your life. I think of my family. I think of several coaches I had growing up. I think of the teachers that impacted my life. I think of all the role models and mentors that I've been blessed to have over the years. Something I've noticed, and I'm sure is true for the people you are thinking about as well, is that all these people have been a source of encouragement in my life.

The sad reality is we live in a world where people are quick to criticize and slow to encourage. Caleb's world wasn't much different. Everyone else was saying there was no way they could conquer the land, even though God already promised it to them (that's why it's called the Promised Land). Everyone was against going into the Promised Land except for Caleb and Joshua. They were like "Don't worry about the people we've got this. We can do it!" Caleb was an encourager.

In-Courage

What exactly does encourage mean? Well, it comes from an old French word, *"encoragier,"* and it is essentially made up of two words. *"En"* meaning "make, or put in" and *"corage"* meaning "courage, heart."[1]

In other words, encourage means to put courage into someone. You give them courage and confidence. On the opposite end, when you discourage someone, you take their courage and confidence away. Caleb tried to put courage into the Israelites so that they could take the Promised Land, and the other spies took their courage away. A different spirit is being an encourager like Caleb. The rest of the world is much like the other spies, full of criticism and discouragement. You may get a couple of laughs when you make a witty comment at someone else's expense. Don't fall into that trap if you want to make a difference. Remember, to make a difference; you must be different.

For the record, there are times when discouragement is appropriate. For example, it is a good idea that you should discourage someone from eating tide pods or sticking their hand on a hot stove. There are a ton of dumb things I've done that I wish someone discouraged me from doing. But, we should actively be encouragers. We should instill courage and confidence in those around us so that they can fulfill God's purpose for their lives.

The world is a harsh place, and you never know what someone is going through. Always assume that someone needs encouragement.

You never know how much it means to someone. One practical thing that I do is if I'm at a restaurant and the service is terrible, I tip more than usual and not less. Of course, your first inclination is to give them what they deserve. But aren't you glad God doesn't treat us how we deserve to be treated? We should give grace to people because of the grace that we have been shown. Don't treat people how they deserve to be treated but treat them how Jesus would treat them.

Paul and Barnabas

In my humble but accurate opinion, the apostle Paul is the greatest missionary of all time. He wrote half of the New Testament, and he planted numerous churches. But, you may not know that Paul had a mentor, a guy named Barnabas. Barnabas played a massive role in Paul's life, and Barnabas believed in Paul when nobody else did. You are probably thinking: "How could there ever have been a time when Paul had people who didn't believe in him?" The guy was a rock star. But, before he followed Jesus, Paul persecuted Christians. He was the unlikeliest of converts and early on, people were skeptical of his salvation.

> *"When he (Paul) arrived in Jerusalem, he tried to join*
> *the disciples, but they were all afraid of him, since they*
> *did not believe he was a disciple. Barnabas, however,*
> *took him and brought him to the apostles and explained*
> *to them how Saul had seen the Lord on the road and*
> *that the Lord had talked to him, and how in Damascus*
> *he had spoken boldly in the name of Jesus."*
> Acts 9:26-27 CSB

Along with Caleb, Barnabas is another example of a great encourager in the Bible. According to Acts 4:36, the name Barnabas means "son of encouragement." God had huge plans to use Paul and to help accomplish those plans; He sent him Barnabas. Why? Because again, everyone needs encouragement.

Barriers to Encouragement

We understand that encouragement is necessary. This probably isn't news to you. But, if we know how important it is, then what hinders us from being the best encouragers we can possibly be? I believe there are a few barriers that often hold us back. You may need to take a good hard look in the mirror to see if you struggle with any of these barriers. Be honest with yourself. If you find one of these barriers applies to you, I can guarantee you aren't alone. I can promise you that because I'm right there with you.

Barrier #1: Self-Centeredness

*"Let each of you look not only to his own
interests, but also to the interests of others."*
Philippians 2:4 ESV

If you are self-centered, you will find it very hard to be an encouraging person. By nature, being an encourager requires you to be other-centered. If you are constantly focused on yourself, you will always overlook people. You just don't notice or care enough to encourage others because it is all about you. A good way to make sure that you never make a difference and that you waste your life is to live a self-centered life. True fulfillment is found in living your life for others. Jesus himself said that He didn't come to be served, but to serve (Mathew 20:28).

Barrier #2: Laziness

"Go to the ant, O sluggard; consider her ways, and be wise."
Proverbs 6:6 ESV

Sometimes, I get ideas about encouraging someone, or I think about reaching out to somebody, and I don't do it. I hope I'm not the only one who does that. Laziness will prevent you from encouraging others. Just thinking about encouraging someone and not having the initiative to do it is useless. What if you were at Starbucks and the person in front of you thought about paying for your coffee? That would probably make your day, right? Wrong! You would never know about it because just thinking about something isn't enough. You must take action to follow through. Try to avoid the barrier of laziness at all costs.

Barrier #3: Busyness

> *"Do not love the world or the things in the world. If anyone*
> *loves the world, the love of the Father is not in him."*
> 1 John 2:15 ESV

On the opposite end of the spectrum from laziness is busyness. If you are too busy, you will also have a hard time encouraging people. You will miss opportunities because you are always in a rush. You must learn to slow down long enough to notice the needs of those around you. Don't be so task-oriented that you lose sight of what is truly important, others. You need to be completely present in your interactions with people and not focused on what you need to be doing next.

Barrier #4: Insecurity

> *"But blessed is the one who trusts in the*
> *Lord, whose confidence is in him."*
> Jeremiah 17:7 NIV

To instill confidence and courage into others, you must first possess those qualities yourself. How can you give someone something that you don't have? Insecurity robs you of your ability to encourage people. Our society is plagued with insecurity. Much of this comes from the fact that we are always comparing ourselves to others. Social media is to blame for much of the comparison madness that goes on today. When you play the comparison game, you will lose every time.

There will always be someone else who is "ahead" of you in some way. Someone will always get more likes than you. Someone will always have a nicer car than you. Someone will always take more vacations than you. Because of Facebook and Instagram, I feel like half of the people I know spend their entire summer at the beach. Don't allow yourself to become insecure because of comparison. If you want to make a difference, you must be secure in yourself. The only you God ever created and ever will create is you.

Motivation for Encouragement

Knowing what holds us back from encouraging others is useful, but we need a way to overcome these barriers. How do we do that? Well, we need to understand what the motivation is that drives encouragement. Dr. Larry Crab says this in his book *Encouragement*:

> *"The only motivation that will stir us to reach into other's lives with encouragement is love."*[2]

The Bible says in John 13:35 that people will know we are disciples of Jesus by the way we love one another. If you don't love someone, you will find it very hard to encourage them. A lack of love for others is the root of all the barriers that were listed. The Bible says in 1 John 4:19 that we love because He first loved us. To love others fully, we must understand that we are fully loved in Jesus.

You are fully known and fully loved by the Creator of the universe. Nobody else can love you exactly like Jesus because nobody else can fully know you. Do you realize that He knows everything you have ever done, everything you have ever thought, and He still decided to go to the cross for you? That is a love like no other. If God loves us like that, how can we not love others? How can we not be serious about encouragement?

Now to be clear, loving others does not mean that you condone the sin in anyone's life. You must be able to speak the truth in love like Jesus did constantly. One of the many examples of this is the woman caught in adultery. Some teachers of the law and Pharisees brought the woman to Jesus ready to stone her, but Jesus told them, "Let him who is without sin among you be the first to throw a stone at her." It is a beautiful picture of God's grace and mercy. But part of that grace and mercy is what Jesus told the woman after this. Jesus did not condemn her, but He told her to "go and leave your life of sin" (John 8:1-11). To be indifferent towards sin is extremely unloving. Loving others like Jesus means telling people what they need to hear instead of what they want to hear. Sincere encouragement done out of love ALWAYS pushes people to be obedient to God's will.

The Power of Encouragement

"Anxiety weighs down the heart, but a kind word cheers it up."
Proverbs 12:25 NIV

"The soothing tongue is a tree of life."
Proverbs 15:4 NIV

*"Gracious words are a honeycomb, sweet to
the soul and healing to the bones."*
Proverbs 16:24 NIV

"The tongue has the power of life and death."
Proverbs 18:21 NIV

The book of Proverbs teaches us that words have an enormous impact. They have the power to build up and the power to tear down. James also talks a lot about the power of words:

"Likewise, the tongue is a small part of the body, but it makes great boasts. Consider what a great forest is set on fire by a small spark. The tongue also is a fire, a world of evil among the parts of the body. It corrupts the whole body, sets the whole course of one's life on fire, and is itself set on fire by hell."
James 3:5-6 NIV

How you talk to people is a big deal. Choose to give people life through your words. It may seem trivial, but it is often the small things in life that make a big difference. The path to different will require you to work hard at controlling your words because how you speak, matters.

One Last Thing

Here's a challenge for you: before you go to sleep tonight, think of one person who is in a tough season or someone who is discouraged. Encourage that person. Visit them, call, text, or whatever you need to do, just encourage that person to the best of your ability. Don't underestimate your ability to make a difference in someone's life. You don't have to be the smartest person in the room or the most athletic to make a difference. You don't need to have the coolest car or the best job. Sometimes, all you need to do to make a difference is be an encourager. Why? Because not a lot of other people are doing it. On the path to different, you are called to have a different spirit like Caleb and like Barnabas.

Discussion

1. Who are some people who have encouraged you?

2. Who in your sphere of influence needs encouragement?

3. How would you want someone to encourage you if you were in a tough situation?

4. What is holding you back from being the best encourager you can be?

5. What comes more natural to you: discouragement or encouragement?

6. Have you ever thought about the power of your words?

7. Discuss some practical ways you can become a better encourager

CHAPTER 3

A DIFFERENT SPIRIT HAS FAITH INSTEAD OF FEAR

*"For God gave us a spirit not of fear but of
power and love and self-control."*
2 Timothy 1:7 ESV

*"Regardless of what you want to do or who you
are, fear will always see you as wholly unqualified
for anything you ever dream or attempt."*[1]
Jon Acuff, author and speaker

When I was younger, I was terrified of riding roller coasters. The first one I ever rode was The Scream Machine at Six Flags Over Georgia. I was in the 4th grade, and my mom had to talk me into it. My advice to you, if you have never ridden a rollercoaster before, is don't start with that one. Back then, the only rides in my comfort zone were the log ride and the whitewater rafting ride. The Scream Machine rocked my world, and I also got my first headache ever that day as well. Back then, I thought I was scared of heights, but now I understand; I didn't trust the rides themselves to keep me safe.

As I got older, my fear of rollercoasters began to fade away, and I will now ride anything. I have even ridden The Scream Machine again several times since then and had tons of fun. What changed? The older I got, the more I realized that roller coasters are generally pretty safe. There are a few exceptions, but millions of people ride them every year with no issue. The fear I once had was replaced with faith. I now have confidence that the rides I go on will keep me safe (knock on wood). Much fear surrounded Caleb.

"But the men who had gone up with him said, 'We can't attack those people; they are stronger than we are.' And they spread among the Israelites a bad report about the land they had explored. They said, 'The land we explored devours those living in it. All the people we saw there are of great size. We saw the Nephilim there (the descendants of Anak come from the Nephilim). We seemed like grasshoppers in our own eyes, and we looked the same to them.'"
Numbers 13: 31-33 NIV

The other spies were terrified of the people who lived in the land they scouted out. The people were bigger and stronger than they were. The odds were stacked against them. They had a spirit of fear. The problem with having a spirit of fear is that you forget God is bigger than what you are afraid of. Notice verse thirty-three again:

"'We saw the Nephilim there (the descendants of Anak come from the Nephilim). We seemed like grasshoppers in our own eyes, and we looked the same to them.'"
Numbers 13:33 NIV

The other spies focused on the size of their enemies. Concentrating on their enemies made them "seem like grasshoppers in their own eyes." However, if they would have thought about how big God is, then maybe this story would have played out differently.

When you dwell on your fears, they always seem larger than they are, and this causes you to feel small and helpless. The good news is that God is bigger than your fears. You may not be strong enough to face them, but He is. Fear will make it very difficult to live a life of purpose and impact, so it is essential to overcome it. How do you do that?

Imagine that there is an empty cup sitting in front of you. Now, remember, it's empty, and there is nothing in it besides air. How do you get the air out? Well, you can't pour the air out, obviously. You must pour something else into the cup, like water. Getting rid of fear is a lot like getting rid of air. To get rid of the fear in your life, you must replace it. The best replacement for fear is faith.

Relax, God's Got This

Fear is not new. Did you know that the first person to ever be afraid was Adam in the Garden of Eden?

> *"He answered, "I heard you in the garden, and I*
> *was afraid because I was naked; so I hid."*
> Genesis 3:10 NIV

When sin entered the world through the fall, fear entered with it. Because of the fall, I know that everyone reading this has experienced fear, is experiencing fear, or is going to experience fear. You are not alone. Even Jesus's disciples experienced fear,

> *That day when evening came, he said to his disciples, 'Let us*
> *go over to the other side.' Leaving the crowd behind, they took*
> *him along, just as he was, in the boat. There were also other*
> *boats with him. A furious squall came up, and the waves*

> *broke over the boat, so that it was nearly swamped. Jesus was
> in the stern, sleeping on a cushion. The disciples woke him
> and said to him, 'Teacher, don't you care if we drown?' He
> got up, rebuked the wind and said to the waves, 'Quiet! Be
> still!' Then the wind died down and it was completely calm.
> He said to his disciples, 'Why are you so afraid? Do you still
> have no faith?' They were terrified and asked each other,
> 'Who is this? Even the wind and the waves obey him!'"*
> Mark 4:35-41 NIV

This passage teaches us a lot about fear. There are four takeaways from this passage that we are going to explore together:

1. When God Is Present, Fear Loses Its Power

The disciples shouldn't have been afraid of the storm. Why? Because they had Jesus in the boat. Jesus is God in the flesh. The author of all, who is in control of everything, including the storm, was there with them. Listen, if you are a child of God, Jesus is with you too. Don't be petrified by the waves crashing into you or jump at the sound of the thunder in your life. The storms in your life are not meant to destroy you. They are intended to push you towards dependence on God.

Charles Spurgeon once said, "I have learned to kiss the waves that throw me against the Rock of Ages."

What an amazing perspective! Whenever you are in a storm, let the waves of trial and suffering throw you against the Rock of Ages. Know that you aren't in the boat alone.

2. The Disciples Had A Promise

> *"That day when evening came, he said to his
> disciples, 'Let us go over to the other side.'"*
> Mark 4:35 NIV

Right here, Jesus promises the disciples that they are going to go to the other side. He didn't say how or in what shape, but when He said let's go to the other side, the disciples should have trusted they would make it somehow. They had a promise to hold on to, but in the chaos of the storm, they had forgotten it.

3. We Have A Promise Too

Before we judge the disciples, we have a promise to hold on to as well. I already hinted towards it by saying Jesus is in your boat, but here is our promise:

> *"He has said, 'I will never leave you nor forsake you.'"*
> Hebrews 13:5 ESV

I don't know what storms you have been through, are going through, or what storms are coming your way. But God does, and He has given you a promise that He is with you and that one day you and I are going to make it to the other side. Jesus tells us in John 14 that He has a place prepared for us:

> *"'Do not let your hearts be troubled. You believe in God; believe also in me. My Father's house has many rooms; if that were not so, would I have told you that I am going there to prepare a place for you? And if I go and prepare a place for you, I will come back and take you to be with me that you also may be where I am. You know the way to the place where I am going.'"*
> John 14:1-4 NIV

All mighty God always keeps His promises. One of the most significant influences on my life, the late Billy Graham, once said, "I've read the last page of the Bible, it's all going to turn out all right." Hold on to that promise!

4. The Cross Is the Power Behind that Promise

God will never leave us or forsake us, and He has a place prepared for us. That's what we are promised. What God never promised us is that we wouldn't experience a storm or that we wouldn't experience pain and suffering in our lives.

So many times, we are like the disciples, "God, do you care?" He does care, and that's why He sent Jesus. My goal here is not to delegitimize the situations that you have faced or are facing in life but to point you to the one who can replace the fear in your life with faith. Because of what Jesus did for us on the cross, and because of His resurrection, we can have faith in His promises. He has been to the other side and has come back to tell us it is okay. One day we will be with Him, free from the fears that plague us in this life.

Keep Your Eyes on Jesus

"Immediately Jesus made the disciples get into the boat and go on ahead of him to the other side, while he dismissed the crowd. After he had dismissed them, he went up on a mountainside by himself to pray. Later that night, he was there alone, and the boat was already a considerable distance from land, buffeted by the waves because the wind was against it. Shortly before dawn Jesus went out to them, walking on the lake. When the disciples saw him walking on the lake, they were terrified. 'It's a ghost,' they said, and cried out in fear. But Jesus immediately said to them: 'Take courage! It is I. Don't be afraid.' 'Lord, if it's you,' Peter replied, 'tell me to come to you on the water.' 'Come,' he said. Then Peter got down out of the boat, walked on the water and came toward Jesus. But when he saw the wind, he was afraid and, beginning to sink, cried out, 'Lord, save me!' Immediately Jesus reached out his hand and caught him. 'You of little faith,' he said, 'why did you doubt?' And when they

climbed into the boat, the wind died down. Then those who were in
the boat worshiped him, saying, 'Truly you are the Son of God.'"
Mathew 14:22-33 NIV

Imagine for a moment what it would be like if you saw someone you know walking on water. It is hard for us to put ourselves in the disciples' shoes because this is the only time in history a situation like this has ever occurred. They think this is some ghost because if it were a person, they would sink. Then, they hear a voice telling them not to be afraid. I'm not sure about you, but if I saw something that I thought was a ghost and then I heard a voice saying don't be scared, I'm probably even more afraid. You've got to hand it to Peter for getting out of the boat. That took some guts.

Peter takes a step. He is now the second person in history to ever walk on water. However, he wasn't focused on this monumental achievement. What he started focusing on was the strength of the wind, and he began to sink.

"Lord, save me!" he exclaimed.

Then, Jesus reaches down and pulls him back up.

"You of little faith, why did you doubt?"

Peter's downfall was when he took his eyes off Jesus. When he stopped focusing on Him, Peter's faith was replaced by fear. Likewise, when we take our eyes off Jesus, we will be filled with fear as well, and we will lack faith like Peter. Stay focused on Him!

Because He Lives

It was the late 1960s, and Bill and Gloria were expecting their third child and were going through a very rough time. Bill was trying to recover from a battle with mono, and Gloria was struggling with terrible anxiety. The thought of bringing another child into this crazy world scared Gloria.

On New Year's Eve, she was sitting in the living room feeling overwhelmed with fear and anxiety about the future. *Time* magazine had just recently published an article called "Is God Dead?" It was a time of extreme racial tension. Drug abuse was rampant everywhere. Then, Gloria unexpectedly began to feel a sense of peace wash over her. The chaos turned to calmness, and she had a realization that the future would be fine because it was all in God's hands.

The baby was born soon after, and Gloria always remembered that moment when her fear was replaced with faith. It was in these circumstances that she and Bill went on to write one of the most famous Christian songs in recent generations.[2] It is a song called "Because He Lives," and here are the lyrics:

> *"God sent His son, they called Him Jesus*
> *He came to love, heal and forgive*
> *He lived and died to buy my pardon*
> *An empty grave is there to prove my Savior lives*
> *Because He lives, I can face tomorrow*
> *Because He lives, all fear is gone*
> *Because I know He holds the future*
> *And life is worth the living, just because He lives*
> *How sweet to hold a newborn baby*
> *And feel the pride and joy He gives*
> *But greater still the calm assurance*
> *This child can face uncertain day, because He lives*
> *Because He lives, I can face tomorrow*
> *Because He lives, all fear is gone*
> *Because I know He holds the future*
> *And life is worth the living, just because He lives*
> *And then one day, I'll cross the river*
> *I'll fight life's final war with pain*
> *And then, as death gives way to victory*

I'll see the lights of glory and I'll know He reigns
Because He lives, I can face tomorrow
Because He lives, all fear is gone
Because I know He holds the future
And life is worth the living, just because He lives
I can face tomorrow
Because He lives, all fear is gone
Because I know He holds the future
And life is worth the living, just because He lives"[3]

Because He lives, you can face whatever tomorrow may bring. You know that even though, tough times will come, and life will sometimes beat you down, God is with you. Let Him steady your nerves and assure your steps. Have faith!

Discussion

1. What were some fears you had growing up?

2. What are some fears that you have now?

3. What are some ways that you deal with fear?

4. Why is it important that we overcome fear?

5. How can you replace the fear in your life with faith?

6. What are some ways that you can keep your eyes on Jesus?

CHAPTER 4

A DIFFERENT SPIRIT SEES POTENTIAL WHEN EVERYONE ELSE SEES A PROBLEM

"Vision is the ability to see potential in what others overlook."[1]
Rick Warren

After our first date, I saw potential, and she saw a problem. I dreamed about the day I would get to marry Taylor, and she was trying to decide how to dump me in the nicest way possible. That is an ideal situation, right? If you are wondering how that worked out, we are now happily engaged to be married. The only explanation I can give to how this happened is the fact that God is good!

All the spies saw the same thing when they scouted out the Promised Land. But while the other spies saw a problem, Caleb saw potential. The other spies saw tremendous obstacles that they thought were impossible to overcome. However, Caleb saw an opportunity to prove to the world that God is the living God who can do impossible things. When everyone else around you is talking about something or someone they view as a problem, look for the potential for God to move in that situation. God specializes in overcoming obstacles.

Jesus was constantly seeing potential in situations while others saw problems. One example of this is found in John 6:

> *"When Jesus looked up and saw a great crowd coming toward him, he said to Philip, 'Where shall we buy bread for these people to eat?' He asked this only to test him, for he already had in mind what he was going to do. Philip answered him, 'It would take more than half a year's wages to buy enough bread for each one to have a bite!' Another of his disciples, Andrew, Simon Peter's brother, spoke up, 'Here is a boy with five small barley loaves and two small fish, but how far will they go among so many?'*
>
> *Jesus said, 'Have the people sit down.' There was plenty of grass in that place, and they sat down (about five thousand men were there). Jesus then took the loaves, gave thanks, and distributed to those who were seated as much as they wanted. He did the same with the fish."*
> John 6:5-11 NIV

Everyone else saw that they had a huge problem: there wasn't enough food to feed everyone. Imagine yourself in this situation; you would be stressed out too. Five thousand hungry people is not something you want to deal with. But while everyone else saw a problem, Jesus saw potential. He saw this as an opportunity to teach everyone that when things seem impossible, there is potential for God to move in a powerful way.

Verse 10 says that there were about five thousand men in attendance. This number leaves out the number of women and children so that number was probably much higher. This miracle serves as an incredible testimony to the power of God to do the seemingly impossible.

Another example of Jesus seeing potential when everyone else saw a problem is found in Luke 19:

> *"Jesus entered Jericho and was passing through. A man was there by the name of Zacchaeus; he was a chief tax collector and was wealthy. He wanted to see who Jesus was, but because he was short he could not see over the crowd. So he ran ahead and climbed a sycamore-fig tree to see him, since Jesus was coming that way.*
>
> *When Jesus reached the spot, he looked up and said to him, 'Zacchaeus, come down immediately. I must stay at your house today.' So he came down at once and welcomed him gladly.*
>
> *All the people saw this and began to mutter, 'He has gone to be the guest of a sinner.'*
>
> *But Zacchaeus stood up and said to the Lord, 'Look, Lord! Here and now I give half of my possessions to the poor, and if I have cheated anybody out of anything, I will pay back four times the amount.'*
>
> *Jesus said to him, 'Today salvation has come to this house, because this man, too, is a son of Abraham. For the Son of Man came to seek and to save the lost.'"*
> Luke 19:1-10 NIV

Ironically, in verse seven, we read that the people were muttering about Jesus going to be the guest of a sinner, while they too were sinners. Back then, tax collectors would often cheat people out of money to make themselves rich. They would overcharge people and keep the profits. Surely, it was a greedy career path for one to follow. It was a good way to make a lot of money but not a good way to make a lot of friends. People wouldn't have liked Zacchaeus since he was a tax collector. They certainly did not see the potential for Jesus to save him that day.

However, while others saw a greedy tax collector that they viewed as a problem, Jesus saw a person in need of grace. He was the only one in the crowd who knew the potential of this situation. Nobody else would have noticed or cared about Zacchaeus sitting in the tree. This goes to show you that just because nobody else sees or notices someone doesn't mean you should overlook them too. Those are the people you should see and notice the most. Jesus had a special heart for the marginalized and forgotten. We should have a heart for them also. This week try to notice people that you might have previously overlooked. Reach out to them and love them like Jesus.

I imagine Zacchaeus being the most shocked out of everyone that Jesus reached out to him. He probably wondered how Jesus knew his name. He probably hadn't had a guest in ages. Jesus met him in his loneliness and despair, and Zacchaeus came out as a child of God. If we, as Christians, are going to be like Jesus, we must follow His example.

Where is it that you need to see potential instead of a problem? Is there someone you think is beyond saving? Is it the environment at school or in the workplace? Do you feel like it's just too bad and you can never make a difference?

In his book *9 Common Lies Christians Believe*, Shane Pruitt, says that one of the biggest lies in Christianity is "Well, _____ will never change."[2] A lot of times, we write people off, and even though we might not say it, we think that person in the blank is just a lost cause. That person will never turn their life around.

Who's in your blank? I'm sure you have someone that comes to mind right now. Maybe, you have more than one person. The good news is that if that person is still breathing and as long as God is still God, there's hope. As Christians, we are all called to share our faith, which is called evangelism.

Evangelism

When was the last time you told someone about Jesus? There is a good possibility you just read that question, and you feel embarrassed. You aren't alone. Maybe you don't feel like you have the ability to share the gospel. Greg Laurie says in his book, *Just Tell Someone:*

> *"No, you may not feel qualified, but God is not looking for ability as much as He is looking for availability. God does not call the qualified; He qualifies the called."*[5]

In God's kingdom, calling is more important than ability. Even if you don't feel qualified, make yourself available. You must be willing to share the hope that you have in Christ with someone. The first time I really told someone about Jesus was my freshman year of college in 2012. I was at a conference called Passion that was held at the Georgia Dome in Atlanta, Georgia. Thousands of college kids go to this conference every year, and I was with my college group from Valley View Baptist Church. It was the first session, and Louie Giglio had just given a message called "No Funeral Today." The passage he used was Luke 7:11-17, where Jesus raises a widow's son on the way to a town called Nain. The message was simple: Jesus is the God who interrupts funerals. He raises the dead to life, and as Christians, we have a message that gives life. This isn't a gift that we should keep to ourselves.

My friend Brandon and I felt convicted by this message, and we prayed for an opportunity to share our faith when we got back home. God didn't wait until that happened. He answered it about thirty minutes later. While walking back to our hotel after the service, we decided to stop and eat somewhere. Suddenly, a feeble looking man approached us and asked if we had any spare cash so he could get some food. You could tell he was genuinely hungry.

We told him that we were actually on the way to eat, and we invited him to come with us. When we got to the food court, we began talking to him about Jesus. We told him how God loved him, and that Jesus died on a cross to save him, and we told him about the resurrection. His eyes started to get watery, he said that he knew a little about Jesus, but nobody had ever taken the time to tell him how he could be saved. We prayed with him and talked to him about salvation some more. He did not make a decision to be saved right then, but he was overwhelmed with gratitude that we cared enough to tell him the good news of Jesus. I believe God used that conversation, and I pray that man has been saved since then.

The funny part about the whole interaction is that Brandon and I specifically mentioned "the mall" when we were praying about sharing our faith. We thought we could go to the mall when we got back home to tell someone about Jesus. After we parted ways, I got chills when we noticed a sign above us at the food court that read, "the mall." Suddenly, we realized that God had answered even that specific part of our prayer! How cool is that?

God moves when we make ourselves available. Live your life on mission. What does that look like? I'm glad you asked.

Living on Mission

Two great examples of people that lived their life on mission are Peter and John. Look at verses 1-4 of Acts chapter 4:

> *"And as they were speaking to the people, the priests and the captain of the temple and the Sadducees came upon them, greatly annoyed because they were teaching the people and proclaiming in Jesus the resurrection from the dead."*
> Acts 4:1-2 ESV

So, Peter and John were out living on mission; they were spreading the gospel. They were taking what Jesus had taught them and teaching other people. Because of their message, the religious leaders approached them with hostility.

The priests were the ones who typically led the services at the temple. They were upset because Peter and John had just healed a lame man back in chapter three, and now, they are out on the temple grounds causing a commotion.

> *"And they arrested them and put them in custody until the next day, for it was already evening. But many of those who had heard the word believed, and the number of the men came to about five thousand."*
> Acts 4:3-4 ESV

Peter and John were impacted by the gospel so much that it launched them into mission. I want you to notice two things about their life on mission that I learned from my mentor and friend, TJ Joy, who is currently the College and Young Adults Pastor at Long Hollow Baptist Church in Hendersonville, Tennessee.

Number 1: Peter and John's Life on Mission Was Motivated by The Resurrection of Jesus

The resurrection of Jesus motivated Peter and John's life on mission. The good news of Jesus changes us. If you look back in Luke 24, you would be amazed that Peter and John are out preaching about Jesus and the resurrection. In Luke 24, a group of women went to the tomb on the third day after Jesus was crucified with spices to take care of the body. When they got to the grave, Jesus was gone. Two angels informed the women that Jesus had risen from the dead.

What happens next is the women run back to the disciples in Luke 24, and they tell them what happened.

They say, "We went to the tomb, and Jesus is not there. Jesus is gone. He is alive. He has risen." When the disciples heard this, they didn't believe them. They thought it was a bunch of rubbish. Then, something miraculous happened. Jesus appeared to them. Jesus appears to the disciples in Luke 24, and even still, they didn't believe. They thought Jesus was some spirit. But then, Jesus shows them His hands and His feet.

He says, "Look, it is me! I am here, I am alive, and I have risen from the dead!"

Their experience with Jesus is what finally convinces them that He has risen. It is after they experience the resurrection that Jesus launches them on mission. He commissions them to go and to tell others the gospel. It was no doubt the resurrection of Jesus that motivated them to go.

Number 2: Peter and John's Life on Mission Helped Generate Addition

In Acts 4:4, Peter and John are preaching about the resurrection when suddenly they are arrested. But, Luke does not fail to mention the effect of their preaching. The number of people that got saved is astounding. Verse 4 says,

> *"But many of those who had heard the word believed, and the number of the men came to about five thousand."*
> Acts 4:4 ESV

The verse says the number of men. Some scholars estimate that including women and children, the number of people who were saved under the teaching of the apostles was over 10,000. Keep in mind this is a time without TV, radio, internet, or social media. This was amazing, and guess what? The word of God STILL has the power to save. My encouragement to you is to remind you that God can use us to save those who need to hear the good news of Jesus. May we be faithful to the word of God and the mission of God.

Nobody is Too Far Gone

When we write someone off because we think they are too far gone for God to save, we are underestimating Jesus's work on the cross. To say that someone's sin is too bad for God to save them is to say that their sin is more powerful than the cross. That is nonsense. The same blood that washed your sins away is powerful enough to wash away the sins of anyone else in the world.

There are no lost causes in the kingdom of God. The person that you don't want to show grace to is the very person you need to give grace to the most. They may not deserve it. That's okay because you didn't either when God gave it to you. When Jesus looked at you, He didn't see a problem. He saw an opportunity to save you, and He took it. The path to different will require you to follow His example, knowing that God's grace has the power to save anyone.

Discussion

1. What potential did Caleb see in the Promised Land?

2. What do you think the people walked away thinking after Jesus fed the five thousand?

3. How do you think Zacchaeus felt when Jesus noticed him?

4. Who have you been overlooking that you need to notice?

5. Have you written anyone off in your life?

6. What holds you back from sharing about Jesus?

7. Who do you need to show grace to in your life?

CHAPTER 5

A DIFFERENT SPIRIT WILL EXPERIENCE OPPOSITION

*"While the whole community threatened to
stone them, the glory of the Lord appeared to
all the Israelites at the tent of meeting."*
Numbers 14:10 CSB

Why is the desire to fit in so strong in most people? Everyone wants to live a life of comfort and ease. As human beings, our natural inclination is to take the path of least resistance. The path to different is not that path. It is full of opposition. Most people hate opposition and crave acceptance. If this is you, I hope that this chapter challenges you and frees you from the bondage of needing to be accepted by everyone.

When you go against the status quo, and you are determined to have a different spirit, you will experience opposition. There is no getting around it. Caleb was determined to be obedient to God by entering the Promised Land. The people responded by wanting to stone him and Joshua. True difference makers don't give up when they come against opposition and criticism. They stand firm in their beliefs, and they will not budge for anyone or anything. Don't get me wrong; I'm not talking about being close-minded. I am talking about having conviction.

Conviction is what gives you strength when you are faced with opposition. If there is one thing this generation desperately needs, it is conviction. You must learn to stand for Jesus even if it offends some people. Not everyone is going to like you. You must love people without compromising the truths found in scripture. Caleb had the conviction that the people needed to be obedient to God, and they needed to go into the Promised Land. Here is what Caleb and Joshua said that landed them in hot water:

> "Then Moses and Aaron fell facedown in front of the whole Israelite assembly gathered there. Joshua son of Nun and Caleb son of Jephunneh, who were among those who had explored the land, tore their clothes and said to the entire Israelite assembly, 'The land we passed through and explored is exceedingly good. If the Lord is pleased with us, he will lead us into that land, a land flowing with milk and honey, and will give it to us. Only do not rebel against the Lord. And do not be afraid of the people of the land, because we will devour them. Their protection is gone, but the Lord is with us. Do not be afraid of them.'"
> Numbers 14:5-9 NIV

Now, I don't know about you, but I've never torn my clothes to get a point across. Caleb and Joshua did just that. There is a culture gap between their time and ours, so this can be hard to understand. But basically, Caleb and Joshua were in extreme despair that the people were about to make a huge mistake. By not entering the land, they were rebelling against the Lord. They reminded the people that God was on their side, and they shouldn't be afraid. What they said infuriated the people, and in response, they wanted to kill Caleb and Joshua. They didn't tell the people what they wanted to hear. They told the people what they needed to hear.

The people wanted to be reaffirmed in their desire not to enter the Promised Land. They stood, once again, on conviction. Often, this is what will bring about opposition towards you. People don't like change, and when you stand for something that interrupts their lives, they don't like it. People like being reaffirmed in their way of life, and they expect you to live the way that they do. When you have a different spirit, you shake things up, and opposition should be expected.

The Forecast for Opposition

"If the world hates you, keep in mind that it hated me first. If you belonged to the world, it would love you as its own. As it is, you do not belong to the world, but I have chosen you out of the world. That is why the world hates you. Remember what I told you: 'A servant is not greater than his master.' If they persecuted me, they will persecute you also. If they obeyed my teaching, they will obey yours also. They will treat you this way because of my name, for they do not know the one who sent me."
John 15:18-21 NIV

If you don't believe me, maybe you will believe Jesus. Scholars commonly call John 13:31-John 17:26, the farewell discourse of Jesus.[1] In other words, it is Jesus's final farewell speech to the apostles, and He is preparing them for life after His ascension to heaven. In John 15:18-21, Jesus gives the apostles, and us, a promise that opposition is in the forecast. It is perfectly normal and expected in the life of a believer.

Tim Challies puts it this way in his blog post titled "Do Not Be Surprised If the World Hates You":

> *"We who follow a hated Savior cannot be surprised*
> *when we experience a measure of his suffering,*
> *when we bear a measure of his shame.*
>
> *But why? Why are we hated? Why is it that we should*
> *be not surprised when the world turns against us?*
>
> *Because Cain hated Abel. Just one verse earlier John has spoken*
> *of these two brothers and asked why one murdered the other.*
> *Cain murdered Abel 'because his own deeds were evil and his*
> *brother's righteous.' Abel's goodness exposed Cain's badness. Abel's*
> *righteousness convicted Cain of his unrighteousness. Abel's love for*
> *God silently declared Cain's disregard. Cain responded with the*
> *ultimate manifestation of hatred—he murdered his own brother.*
>
> *Your goodness unmasks the badness of the unbelievers*
> *around you. Your light illumines their darkness.*
>
> *Christian, you must expect to be hated today for the same*
> *reason. Your goodness unmasks the badness of the unbelievers*
> *around you. Your light illumines their darkness. Your truth*
> *exposes their error. Your holiness declares their depravity.*
> *Your life stands in judgment of them, it convicts them of*
> *their guilt, it shows them who God expects them to be."*[2]

If we were just a part of the world, if we just fit in, then the world would love us as its own. But, because we do not belong to the world, because we are different, the world hates us. Now, this doesn't mean that the goal is to get everyone to hate you. You can quickly get everyone to not like you by just being a miserable person to be around. Don't do that. Your goal is to make a difference by having a different spirit. Opposition will come, but you will have the peace of mind that Jesus Himself experienced opposition too, and He promised it would happen.

Forecast Fulfilled

Jesus told the apostles that they would experience opposition, and He was right. All the apostles, besides John, were eventually killed for their faith. But even though John wasn't killed, he still had his fair share of persecution by being imprisoned on the island of Patmos as a result of anti-Christian persecution under the Roman emperor Domitian. The first Christians were brutally persecuted, and many of them were killed. It was under these conditions that the early church grew like wildfire. Tertullian, an early church father, coined this phrase in his most famous work, *Apologeticus*:

> *"The blood of the martyrs is the seed of the Church."*[5]

The persecution of the early church had the opposite effect that the Romans intended. They killed people for being Christians, but others would see their faith and became Christians themselves. Why would anyone do such a thing knowing the risk involved?

Others saw something different in these Christians. These early Christians knew that their opposition and suffering wasn't in vain. God was using their persecution for His glory. Did you know there is still plenty of persecution going on in the world today? There are many countries where you can be killed for becoming a Christian. However, much like with the early church, these tend to be the countries where Christianity is spreading like wildfire.

God uses all things for His glory. Whatever opposition the world may throw your way is no match for God. He won't let it be in vain.

When the world doesn't accept you, you can rest in the fact that God completely accepts you because of what Jesus has done on the cross. The path to different is paved with difficulty.

Responding to Opposition

Now that we know opposition is coming, what should our response be? The prophet Nehemiah had the massive task of rebuilding the walls in Jerusalem that were destroyed by the Babylonian king Nebuchadnezzar. When God gives you a huge task, you can bet opposition is coming your way. This is what happened with Nehemiah. We read about his opposition in Nehemiah 4 along with his response:

> *"Now when Sanballat heard that we were building the wall,*
> *he was angry and greatly enraged, and he jeered at the Jews.*
> *And he said in the presence of his brothers and of the army of*
> *Samaria, 'What are these feeble Jews doing? Will they restore it*
> *for themselves? Will they sacrifice? Will they finish up in a day?*
> *Will they revive the stones out of the heaps of rubbish, and burned*
> *ones at that?' Tobiah the Ammonite was beside him, and he said,*
> *'Yes, what they are building—if a fox goes up on it he will break*
> *down their stone wall!' Hear, O our God, for we are despised.*
> *Turn back their taunt on their own heads and give them up to be*
> *plundered in a land where they are captives. Do not cover their*
> *guilt, and let not their sin be blotted out from your sight, for*
> *they have provoked you to anger in the presence of the builders.*
> *So we built the wall. And all the wall was joined together*
> *to half its height, for the people had a mind to work."*
> Nehemiah 4:1-6 ESV

When Nehemiah faced this extreme opposition, he kept on working, and he kept on doing what God had called him to do.

When opposition comes your way, you must do the same. You must keep on working and doing what God has called YOU to do. Don't wait for permission. If you sit around waiting to please everyone, you will never accomplish anything. Do not let opposition paralyze you. Be active in fulfilling the purpose that God has for your life.

Thank You, Lord! I Know I Still Have Your Presence

J. G. Morrison is credited with telling this story about the great preacher, John Wesley:

> "John Wesley was riding along on his horse one day when he realized that three days had passed, and he had not been persecuted in any way. Not a single brick or egg had been thrown in his direction. So, he stopped his horse and said out loud, "Could it be that I am backslidden, or I have sinned?" Slipping down from his horse, he knelt on one knee and asked the Lord to show him if there was anything wrong with him spiritually.
>
> A man who disliked Wesley saw him kneeling in prayer, so he picked up a brick and threw it at him, barely missing the preacher. When Wesley saw the brick fly by, he said, 'Thank you, Lord! I know I still have Your presence.'"[4]

I used to think that if someone didn't like me that there was something wrong with me. Now, I know that it is normal. It is a rite of passage for believers if you will. Following Jesus will cost you something. It may cost you something different than it does me, but it will cost you something, nonetheless. If you think about it, our faith in Jesus must cost us something so that we can realize that Jesus is worth more than whatever that something is.

How do you push through the opposition? Notice what John Wesley said, "Thank you, Lord! I know I still have your presence." God is with you. That is how you face the opposition in your life. The God of the entire universe, the Creator of all things, has your back. You can face anything coming your way because He is with you. Don't give up when things get tough. Stay on the path to different. At the end of the road, you will look back and realize that God was using the stones thrown at you for His purposes. Furthermore, He is using them to make you look more like Jesus.

Discussion

1. In what areas do you struggle with the desire to fit in?

2. What are your thoughts on John 15:18-21?

3. In what ways have you personally experienced opposition?

4. How will you respond to opposition in the future?

5. How can you be there for others experiencing opposition?

CHAPTER 6

A DIFFERENT SPIRIT HAS A SENSE OF URGENCY

"But Caleb quieted the people before Moses and said, "Let us go
up at once and occupy it, for we are well able to overcome it."
Numbers 13:30 ESV

Can you feel the urgency in Caleb's voice? Let us go up AT ONCE. People with a different spirit recognize that time is the most valuable resource that we have. No amount of money on earth can buy you one more second. Think about that. Every moment that goes by is gone forever. If you are going to make a difference, you too must live with a sense of urgency. You don't have forever. God has given you a mission. Your mission is called the great commission, and here it is:

> *"And Jesus came and said to them, 'All authority in heaven*
> *and on earth has been given to me. Go therefore and make*
> *disciples of all nations, baptizing them in the name of the*
> *Father and of the Son and of the Holy Spirit, teaching*

> *them to observe all that I have commanded you. And*
> *behold, I am with you always, to the end of the age.'"*
> Mathew 28:18-20 ESV

Christians should be the most urgent people on the planet. Michael Kelly in his blog titled "3 Things That Keep Christians From Living with A Sense of Urgency" says,

> *"Christians are meant to live with a sense of urgency. Urgency is not*
> *panic, anxiety, or acting before we think; it is a sense of insistence*
> *that requires steady, and often swift, action. But why is that? The*
> *answer, of course, is simple – it's because the message of the gospel*
> *is a message of urgency. Before we come to understand the good*
> *news of Jesus Christ, we must come to understand the grave news*
> *of sin. Whether we know it or not, all of us are in the most real*
> *and the most grave danger apart from the gospel. Not one of us*
> *knows which breath will be our last, which sunrise will be the final*
> *one we see, which phone call will signal the end of our days."*

The world is in danger, and it doesn't even realize it. As Christians, we have the news that could save it. How can we go about business as usual with this knowledge? Not having a sense of urgency is catastrophic to the world around us. This statement is extremely cliché, but tomorrow is never promised. Don't put off tomorrow what needs to be done today. Go out and make an impact.

Complacency: The Enemy of Urgency

The thing that holds most people back from living a life that makes a difference for the kingdom of God is complacency. We so easily fall into the trap of routine. We are so used to doing the same thing every week. We go to church once maybe twice a week, but that's it. We give God His two hours, and the rest of the week is ours for the taking.

Don't fall for that! Following Christ involves every hour of your week. Let God interrupt your life to use you to accomplish His will. Whatever you do, don't become complacent because it robs you of your passion. Passion is the fuel for your purpose. Without passion for God, you will never realize His purpose for your life. God has work for you to do.

Good Works

"For we are God's handiwork, created in Christ Jesus to do good works, which God prepared in advance for us to do."
Ephesians 2:8-10 NIV

Did you catch that? If you are a child of God, there is no room for complacency because there are good works out there for you to do. It is important to understand that good works do not save you; we are saved by faith. But you are saved FOR good works.

Good works are more than just nice deeds, and the goal is more than just being a good person. Anyone can be a generally kind and good person by worldly standards. You don't have to be a Christian to do nice things. But you do have to be a Christian to live a life that glorifies God. The "good works" we are talking about are the works that glorify God and bring people to Jesus.

1. Good works flow out of having a relationship with God

When Jesus went to the cross and saved us from our sins, He was also making it possible for us to have a relationship with the Father. We must understand that the fall in Genesis 3 did more damage than we could ever realize. It completely destroyed our relationship with God. It separated us from Him. What Jesus did on the cross is He restored our relationship to God that was broken by sin. If you call yourself a Christian, you have access to the presence of God, and the more you are in the presence of God, the more you will be changed. Good works will flow out of you because the more you are with someone, the more you become like that person, right?

We start to look like who we spend time with, and if we aren't spending time with God, then it will be very hard to do much that glorifies Him. The Bible says it like this:

> *"I am the vine; you are the branches. If you remain in me and I in you, you will bear much fruit; apart from me you can do nothing."*
> John 15:5 NIV

We can do nothing apart from God. Look at the focus in this verse. It's saying if you remain in me, if you abide in me, if you have a relationship with me, then you WILL bear much fruit. It doesn't say we might bear much fruit; it says we will bear much fruit. What is the fruit that the Bible is talking about? Well, in Galatians 5:22-23, we are told:

> *"But the fruit of the Spirit is love, joy, peace, patience, kindness, goodness, faithfulness, gentleness and self-control."*
> Galatians 5:22-23 ESV

The work of God should be present in the lives of every person who calls themselves a Christian. Nobody is perfect, but if a person lives a lifestyle of habitual sin and they never have any real change in their lives, then there is a good chance they aren't just backslidden, but they are still lost. What would the people closest to you say if they were asked if you had these traits?

Are you loving? Are you joyful? Are you peaceful? Are you patient? Are you kind? Are you good? Are you faithful? Are you gentle? Do you have self-control?

2. Good works are a response to God's Word

Over and over studies and research shows that out of all the spiritual disciplines that Bible intake is consistently the number one indicator in determining spiritual health. It impacts all of the other disciplines. In other words, reading the Bible affects how we live our lives. Show me the godliest person you know, and I guarantee you they will have a marked-up Bible that they read every day.

"No work can be good unless it is commanded by God"
Charles Spurgeon

How do you know what God commands if you never listen to His voice? One of the most common questions I get is, "I feel like God is silent. How can I hear from God?" The Bible is the Word of God, and when it is open, and you are reading it, God is speaking to you. That is how you hear God speak. 2 Timothy 3:16-17 says,

"All Scripture is God-breathed and is useful for teaching, rebuking, correcting and training in righteousness, so that the servant of God may be thoroughly equipped for every good work."
Timothy 3:16-17 NIV

The Bible is what equips us for every good work. You can't expect to live the life God has called you to live with a closed Bible on your nightstand. When Jesus Himself was tempted by Satan in the desert, the weapon that he used to withstand temptation was scripture. To every temptation, Jesus responded with the phrase "It is written," Check out this conversation between Jesus and Satan to see what I mean:

"Then Jesus was led by the Spirit into the wilderness to be tempted by the devil. After fasting forty days and forty nights,

he was hungry. The tempter came to him and said, 'If you
are the Son of God, tell these stones to become bread.' Jesus
answered, 'It is written: 'Man shall not live on bread alone,
but on every word that comes from the mouth of God.'"
Mathew 4:1-4 NIV

3. Good works bring credibility to our testimony

We've all heard the saying: "actions speak louder than words." What that saying means is that if our actions don't back up our words, then our words don't mean anything. Good works give credibility to us when we share the gospel. People are a lot more open to us when our actions back up our words. When we tell people that we are Christians but live like the world; it destroys our testimony.

Your testimony is just your story about how God has saved you and changed your life. Don't let the way you live make you ineffective for the kingdom of God. But instead, live in a way that when you tell people about God, they want to hear what you say. The world needs to see a difference in us. It needs to see that God still changes lives.

Grace Inspired Urgency

Good works are a response to the fact that God has done a work in our lives. The fuel that powers the urgency behind those good works is grace. If you lack a sense of urgency in your walk with God, chances are the grace in your fuel tank is running low. God's amazing grace should always amaze us. Until you fill your tank back up, you will lack motivation, and you will struggle along in a place of complacency.

The gospel, or the good news of Jesus, is not just what saves you. It is what motivates you to live the Christian life. That means it is not only the unsaved person that needs to hear the gospel but saved people need the gospel too. You will never outgrow the gospel. Find time every day to remind yourself of what Jesus did for you on the cross. He lived the life you should have lived, and He died the death you should have died. However, He didn't stay dead. He rose to life again to make a way for you to have a relationship with Him.

A New Day

Legendary coach, Paul Bear Bryant, carried a poem around in his wallet called "A New Day" that he often read to his players. Here is the poem:

> "This is the beginning of a new day. God has given me this
> day to use as I will. I can waste it or use it for good. What I
> do today is very important because I am exchanging a day of
> my life for it. When tomorrow comes, this day will be gone
> forever, leaving something in its place I have traded for it.
> I want it to be gain, not loss—good, not evil. Success, not
> failure in order that I shall not forget the price I paid for it."[2]
> Heartsill Wilson

Whatever day it is that you are reading this, make the most of it. You will never get this day back, use it for good and don't waste it. On the path to different, you must have an intense sense of urgency if you are going to make a difference for the kingdom of God. You must confront the complacency in your life head-on. You must deal with it every morning when you wake up by remembering that each day is a gift from God that He intends for you to use for His glory.

Discussion

1. Why do you think Caleb had such a sense of urgency about going into the Promised Land?

2. In what ways do you need to work on your time management skills?

3. Would you describe yourself as having a sense of urgency?

4. In your words, why is complacency the enemy to urgency?

5. What are some examples of good works?

6. Why is it grace that inspires urgency?

7. How can you use this day for good and not waste it?

CHAPTER 7

A DIFFERENT SPIRIT HAS
THE HOLY SPIRIT

"Without the Spirit of God, we can do nothing.
We are as ships without wind. We are useless."
Charles Spurgeon

The first time I ever preached in front of a large crowd was several years ago as an intern with the student ministry at First Baptist Church Woodstock in Woodstock, Georgia. I was a nervous wreck. I honestly didn't think I could do it. I'm not going to say I thought about faking sick to get out of it, but I'm not saying I didn't either. What made it worse is that I practiced my message in front of some of the other student ministry staff the day before, and it went TERRIBLE. I'm embarrassed just thinking about it. The whole situation was shaping up for disaster.

The next day, I thought I was going to vomit. But then the moment came. I made it through the opening worship songs without passing out, amazingly. It was time for me to deliver my first message. The weirdest thing happened as I walked out on the platform, a wave of peace and boldness like I've never felt before. Don't get me wrong. I was still nervous. If you were to ask the people that heard that message, they would tell you I was. But the more I began to speak, the more boldness I felt. I was saying stuff I wasn't planning on saying, and it was way better than anything I had expected. It wasn't a Billy Graham sermon, by any means, and droves of kids didn't get saved. But that night, I felt the power of the Holy Spirit in my weakness.

I can go on and on about ways you can be different, but the fact of the matter is that it's God who gives us a different spirit when we put our trust in Jesus. The spirit that He gives us is the Holy Spirit. His role in your life is crucial.

The Holy Spirit is given to everyone who is a child of God, and He is what enables us to live the Christian life. The Bible says in Romans 8 that the same spirit that raised Jesus from the dead lives inside of US. But here's the problem, we are supposed to have the same spirit that raised Jesus from the dead, but the nasty truth is that sometimes we live like He is still in the grave. If we are going to take the path to different, we must allow the Holy Spirit to work in and through us.

Wayne Grudem in his book *Systematic Theology* defines the work of the Holy Spirit like this:

> *"The work of the Holy Spirit is to manifest the active presence of God in the world, and especially in the church."*

Have you ever talked to someone and felt like God spoke to you through that person? Or have you ever spoken to someone and walked away feeling like God gave you the exact words to say like I did in my first message? You thought to yourself: "Where did that come from?" Many times, that's the Holy Spirit. Now, sometimes that's not the case. Someone might tell you God told them to say or do something, yet it's just them using God for authority. Sometimes, people use this as a manipulation tactic, which is sickening. But the truth is that the Holy Spirit is at work all around us. You can write a whole book on the Holy Spirit, and many have. In this chapter, we are just going to explore the four jobs of the Holy Spirit:

1. The Holy Spirit Gives Power

> *"But you will receive power when the Holy Spirit has come upon you, and you will be my witnesses in Jerusalem and in all Judea and Samaria, and to the end of the earth."*
> Acts 1:8 ESV

Check out this example in Acts 4:

> *"On the next day their rulers and elders and scribes gathered together in Jerusalem, with Annas the high priest and Caiaphas and John and Alexander, and all who were of the high-priestly family. And when they had set them in the midst, they inquired, 'By what power or by what name did you do this?' Then Peter, filled with the Holy Spirit, said to them, 'Rulers of the people and elders,'"*
> Acts 4:5-8 ESV

Peter was filled with the Holy Spirit. But way before this happened, Jesus prepared him for this moment:

> *"And when they bring you before the synagogues and the rulers and the authorities, do not be anxious about how you should defend yourself or what you should say, for the Holy Spirit will teach you in that very hour what you ought to say."*
> Luke 12:11-12 ESV

Jesus said, "Listen, you are going to be brought in. You are going to be persecuted. But I want you at this moment not to depend on yourself but to depend on the Holy Spirit." The Holy Spirit is the power inside of us.

If you are over the age of sixteen, you probably know the feeling of getting into your car, cranking it, and then nothing happens. It isn't a good feeling. One of the first times this happened to me was one day after school in the tenth grade. What happened is I left my lights on that morning because it was raining, and then after school, the battery in my truck was dead as a doornail. My power source was gone, and until I got it back, I wasn't going anywhere. Luckily, one of my friends had some jumper cables, and I was able to get it cranked right back up. The Holy Spirit is our power source, and without Him, we are as powerless as a vehicle with no battery.

2. The Holy Spirit Convicts

> *"And when He comes, He will convict the world*
> *concerning sin and righteousness and judgment:"*
> John 16:8 ESV

Have you ever felt convicted over your sin? You have the Holy Spirit to thank for that. None of us are perfect, but one way that you know you are a Christian is that after you sin, you feel the conviction of the Holy Spirit. If you feel no such conviction, then you should highly question your salvation. True believers don't celebrate sin. A Christian can't be comfortable with the sin in their life that sent Jesus to the cross. Jesus loves you as you are, but He also loves you enough not to leave you as you are. When the Holy Spirit convicts us, it leads to repentance.

The word "repentance" means to turn from your sin. It is not just feeling sad about your sin. The rich young ruler that asked Jesus what he needed to do to inherit eternal life walked away sad when

Jesus told him to sell all his possessions and give them to the poor. Even though he was sad about his sin of greed, he was still lost after this encounter. Don't think that just because you've felt sorry about your sin before that you are in a right relationship with God. You must turn from your sin and turn to Jesus. This will be a lifelong struggle, but you must never be okay with the sin in your life. Yes, we are all sinners, and none of us are perfect. But the fact that God's grace covers us when we sin should make us sin less and not more. Paul addresses this issue in Romans 6:

> "What should we say then? Should we continue in sin so that grace may multiply? Absolutely not! How can we who died to sin still live in it? Or are you unaware that all of us who were baptized into Christ Jesus were baptized into his death? Therefore, we were buried with him by baptism into death, in order that, just as Christ was raised from the dead by the glory of the Father, so we too may walk in newness of life."
> Romans 6:1-4 CSB

At the moment of salvation, you die to sin, and you are raised to walk in newness of life. You can't walk in the newness of life if you are still doing the same old things you did before you met Jesus. Sure, you will always struggle with sin. However, when you struggle as a Christian, the Holy Spirit is there to convict you and give you the power to overcome your sin. If you don't destroy the sin in your life, the sin in your life will destroy you.

3. The Holy Spirit Leads

> "For all who are led by the Spirit of God are sons of God."
> Romans 8:14 ESV

It is the Holy Spirit that leads you through life if you are a child of God. You never have to wander through life alone. How amazing is that? The fact that the Holy Spirit leads you should cause you to seek His guidance in your day to day life.

I couldn't imagine traveling places I've never been without a map, whether it be Google maps, Apple maps, or even just an old-fashioned map. If none of those existed, travel would be extremely challenging. It would be so hard to get places. The Holy Spirit navigates us through life. He shows us the way we should go. Going through life without Him is like traveling very far away without a map to show you the way.

4. The Holy Spirit is Your Advocate, Comforter, and Helper

"But the Advocate, the Holy Spirit, whom the Father
will send in my name, will teach you all things and
will remind you of everything I have said to you."
John 14:26 NIV

"But the Comforter, which is the Holy Ghost,
whom the Father will send in my name, he shall
teach you all things, and bring all things to your
remembrance, whatsoever I have said unto you."
John 14:26 KJV

"But the Helper, the Holy Spirit, whom the Father will
send in my name, he will teach you all things and bring
to your remembrance all that I have said to you."
John 14:26 ESV

One verse, three words, which one is right? Well, all of them. Each of these words comes from the Greek word "*parakletos.*" This word can be translated into all three of these words. He supports you as an advocate. He comforts you when you grieve. He is a constant source of help and guidance. In other words, you need the Holy Spirit.

The Holy Spirit and the Path to Different

The path to different without the Holy Spirit is not just hard; it's impossible. Without Him, it is impossible to live the Christian life. You won't get very far at all by yourself. When you are filled with the Holy Spirit, it is impossible not to be different, and it is impossible for the world not to notice this difference. It is this difference that the world sees in you that allows you to make a difference. It is how you live a life that impacts. Part of God's purpose in your life is for the Holy Spirit to show His power in your weakness.

Discussion

1. What comes to mind when you think about the Holy Spirit?

2. Have you ever experienced the Holy Spirit working in your life?

3. What do you think about the Holy Spirit convicting us?

4. In what ways do you think that the Holy Spirit leads us?

5. What is your response to the Holy Spirit being your advocate, comforter, and helper?

CHAPTER 8

A DIFFERENT SPIRIT IS OBEDIENT TO GOD

"But because my servant Caleb has a different spirit and follows me wholeheartedly, I will bring him into the land he went to, and his descendants will inherit it."
Numbers 14:24 NIV

"It's not the truth that you know, but the truth you obey that matters"
Dr. Johnny Hunt

Caleb had a different spirit because he followed God wholeheartedly. In other words, he was determined to be obedient to God. The rest of the Israelites were disobedient. God told them to take the Promised Land, and they didn't want to do it. You see, sin isn't always an action; sometimes, it is inaction. When God has called you to do something, and you refuse to do it, that is a sin. Having a different spirit involves taking action. God has a purpose for you, and if you are not obedient to Him, you are missing out on that purpose. But what does that look like?

The Obedience God Desires

I don't watch much TV, but one type of show I like is true crime. I enjoy mystery. One of the things I've learned from watching crime shows is that one of the first things detectives do when someone commits a crime is try to figure out the motive. This chapter, I want you to think about your motives behind your obedience to God. Why do you read your Bible? Why do you pray? Why do you go to church?

You see, there's a motivation behind every evil deed ever done, but there is also a motivation behind every good thing ever done. So, what is the obedience that God desires and what is the motivation for following Him that He is looking for?

> *"Not everyone who says to me, 'Lord, Lord,' will enter the kingdom of heaven, but the one who does the will of my Father who is in heaven. On that day many will say to me, 'Lord, Lord, did we not prophesy in your name, and cast out demons in your name, and do many mighty works in your name?' And then will I declare to them, 'I never knew you; depart from me, you workers of lawlessness.'"*
> Mathew 7:21-23 NIV

Dean Inserra says this in his book *The Unsaved Christian*:

> *"Consider the petitions Jesus gave as an example in*
> *Mathew 7:21-23 in our modern context. I believe*
> *His examples would translate to our era like this:*
> *Didn't we 'say grace' before dinner?*
> *Didn't we vote our values?*
> *Didn't we believe prayer should be allowed in school?*
> *Didn't we go to church?*
> *Didn't we believe in God?*

Didn't we get misty eyes whenever we heard 'God Bless America'
Didn't we give money to the church?
Didn't we treat women with respect?
Didn't we own Bibles?
Didn't we get the baby chastened by the priest?
Didn't we want America to return to its Christian roots?
Didn't we stay married and faithful?"[1]

Just because you are good at behaving like a Christian doesn't mean you are a Christian. Don't be deceived into believing you are something that you are not. God isn't just after your obedience, but He is after your heart behind the obedience, which is why it is so important to talk about the obedience that God desires. But first, we need to talk about obedience that He doesn't desire.

1. Obedience that wants something from God

When I was a kid, I knew exactly what it took to get something from my parents. If I wanted a new toy or something, I wouldn't immediately ask for it. First, I would make sure I minded my parents very well that day. If they asked me to clean my room, I would clean it. I may have even cleaned it without them asking. Then and only then, after I buttered them up, I would ask for what I wanted.

Some people are obedient to God for this very reason. Outwardly these people look very good, but inwardly, they are basically just treating God like Santa Clause. They are trying to get on the nice list, so God gives them what they want. The Bible says this about these kinds of people:

> *"You ask and do not receive, because you ask*
> *wrongly, to spend it on your passions."*
> James 4:3 ESV

The problem with this kind of obedience is that it is an attempt to twist the arm of God into blessing you because you've been so good and obedient. This is an "if I do this, you must do that" mentality. This is obviously not a good motivation for being obedient to God.

One widespread belief is that if someone goes to church and gives money, then God won't interfere with their life too much the rest of the week. In other words, it doesn't matter how that person lives their life the rest of the week if they show up to church every Sunday. God does bless your church attendance and your giving, but those things should reflect your obedience throughout the rest of the week.

When we obey God, there is no negotiating. We don't deserve anything from Him. Some of you might be thinking well, that's not fair. I want what I deserve: no, you don't. You don't want what you deserve because if we got what we deserve, then we would have been the ones who went to the cross.

2. Obedience that wants to be seen by others

The best example of this is the Pharisees:

> *"Jesus goes on, "They do all their deeds to be seen by others""*
> Matthew 23:5 ESV

The Pharisees prayed to be seen by others:

> *"And when you pray, do not be like the hypocrites,*
> *for they love to pray standing in the synagogues and*
> *on the street corners to be seen by others. Truly I tell*
> *you, they have received their reward in full."*
> Mathew 6:5 NIV

They served the poor to be seen by others:

*"So, when you give to the needy, do not announce it
with trumpets, as the hypocrites do in the synagogues
and on the streets, to be honored by others."*
Matthew 6:2 NIV

They obeyed the scriptures to be seen by others:

*"Be careful not to practice your righteousness
in front of others to be seen by them."*
Matthew 6:1 NIV

They received exactly what they wanted: recognition and esteem from others. But obedience that wants to be seen by others is obedience that does not know Jesus. If you have Jesus, you do not need to be seen by others. You should not do the things that you do for anyone besides God.

3. Obedience that is self-righteous

Charles Spurgeon said:

*"The greatest enemy to human souls is the self-righteous
spirit which makes men look to themselves for salvation."*

Read Mathew 7:22 again:

*"Many will say to me on that day, 'Lord, Lord, did we
not prophesy in your name and in your name drive out
demons and in your name perform many miracles?"*
Mathew 7:22 NIV

Notice, it is all about what they have done. A mindset like this is a sign of self-righteousness. Instead of it being all about what Jesus has done, the focus becomes all about you. Nowhere in this verse did they say did anyone mention trusting in Jesus. Because they didn't trust in Jesus, they trusted in themselves.

Paul talks about this extensively in the book of Galatians. We find out some teachers have come along telling the Galatians that they need to focus more on their righteousness and that it was a part of their salvation. But we are saved by grace alone through faith and not by anything that we do. We aren't saved by our righteousness but by the righteousness of Jesus. This is Paul's argument in a nutshell.

> *"I do not set aside the grace of God, for if righteousness could be gained through the law, Christ died for nothing!"*
> Galatians 2:21 NIV

You can never be good enough to make it to heaven on your own righteousness. You will never be good enough to stand guiltless before a holy God. We need the righteousness of Jesus. So, we have talked about the wrong kinds of obedience. What is the obedience God desires?

Obedience That Comes from Loving Jesus

Our obedience isn't what saves us. It's not about building your reputation, and it's not a way to arm-twist God into giving you something. Our obedience should be an overflow of our relationship with Jesus. The truth is heaven isn't full of people who fear hell. Heaven is full of people who love Jesus. But I can't make you love Jesus; all I can do is tell you what He's done for you and that He loves you.

When the Bible said that Caleb followed God, it said he did so wholeheartedly. Caleb was following God with his heart because he loved God and desired to do His will. This is the obedience God desires and the obedience that comes from someone with a different spirit.

Everyone Is Obedient to Something

The word "obedient" might rub you the wrong way. You might think of yourself as a free spirit that likes to do stuff your way. You might think that you are independent, and you don't follow anyone or anything. You are obedient to no one in your mind. But the only problem with that way of thinking is whether you realize it or not you are obedient to something.

If you aren't obedient to God, then you will place your devotion and obedience on something else. Maybe it is your job. It is your life. When your job calls, you answer, and everything else in your life takes a back seat. You could be obedient to an addiction. You may think of yourself as a rebel who isn't obedient to anyone, yet you are a slave to some sort of addiction in your life. There are so many examples I could put here, but the point is that if you aren't obedient to God, you will be obedient to something else. The Bible puts it like this in Romans 6:

> *"Don't you know that if you offer yourselves to someone as obedient slaves, you are slaves of that one you obey—either of sin leading to death or of obedience leading to righteousness?"*
> Romans 6:16 CSB

According to this verse, when we are obedient to God, it leads to life, and when we are obedient to sin, it leads to death. The catch is that if we are obedient to anything else besides God, it is a sin because He is the only One worthy of our obedience. The path to different will require you to put your ego aside and to recognize that the Author of life knows what is best. Caleb understood this. You must follow his example by being obedient to God's will for your life. This obedience is what will make it possible for you to live a life of purpose and impact.

Discussion

1. What are your thoughts on Mathew 7:21-23? What is your response?

2. Do you struggle with any of these wrong kinds of obedience?

3. What are some ways you can strengthen your love for Jesus?

4. Is there anything in your life that you are obeying besides Jesus?

CHAPTER 9

A DIFFERENT SPIRIT LEADS OTHERS TOWARDS GOD

*"Only do not rebel against the Lord. And do not
fear the people of the land, for they are bread for
us. Their protection is removed from them, and
the Lord is with us; do not fear them."*
Numbers 14:9 ESV

The people were rebelling against God by not going into the Promised Land, and Caleb tried to stop them. He was trying to lead the people towards God. That is what a person with a different spirit does. We must be mindful that in every interaction with others, we are either pulling them towards God or away. You are influencing others everywhere you go. If you are to fulfill your purpose and live a life of impact, you must have a different spirit like Caleb. This means leveraging whatever influence you have to point others towards Jesus.

A Tale of Two Kings

Hezekiah was 25 years old when he became king of Judah. He had very small shoes to fill because his father, Ahaz, was a terrible king. Hezekiah's name means "God has strengthened." This is fitting because he did a lot of good as king. He reversed a lot of the evil that his father did. He reinstated Passover as a national holiday. He brought back the Levitical priesthood. He also restored proper worship. Hezekiah even said a prayer one time that God answered by sending an angel to kill 185,000 Assyrians. This prayer saved Jerusalem.[1]

According to 2 Kings 18, Hezekiah was a good king who did what was right in the sight of the Lord, just like King David. For the most part, he led the kingdom towards God. But, like David, Hezekiah wasn't perfect. He got sick later in life and prayed for God to heal him. God answered this prayer by giving Hezekiah fifteen more years to live. It was in these last fifteen years that he showed off all of his wealth and treasure to the Babylonians. Isaiah called him a fool and foretold that the Babylonians would eventually take away everything that he had shown off to them. It was also during this fifteen-year period that he had a son, Manasseh.

We first meet Manasseh in 2 Kings 21:1-2:

> *"Manasseh was twelve years old when he began to reign, and*
> *he reigned fifty-five years in Jerusalem. His mother's name*
> *was Hephzibah. And he did what was evil in the sight of*
> *the Lord, according to the despicable practices of the nations*
> *whom the Lord drove out before the people of Israel."*
> *2 Kings 21:1-2 ESV*

The apple fell far from the tree with Manasseh. He was a very wicked king and he leads the people away from God instead of towards him. This is his legacy that 2 Kings 21 gives us:

"For he rebuilt the high places that Hezekiah his father had destroyed, and he erected altars for Baal and made an Asherah, as Ahab king of Israel had done, and worshiped all the host of heaven and served them. And he built altars in the house of the Lord, of which the Lord had said, 'In Jerusalem will I put my name.' And he built altars for all the host of heaven in the two courts of the house of the Lord. And he burned his son as an offering and used fortune-telling and omens and dealt with mediums and with necromancers. He did much evil in the sight of the Lord, provoking him to anger. And the carved image of Asherah that he had made he set in the house of which the Lord said to David and to Solomon his son, 'In this house, and in Jerusalem, which I have chosen out of all the tribes of Israel, I will put my name forever. And I will not cause the feet of Israel to wander anymore out of the land that I gave to their fathers, if only they will be careful to do according to all that I have commanded them, and according to all the Law that my servant Moses commanded them.' But they did not listen, and Manasseh led them astray to do more evil than the nations had done whom the Lord destroyed before the people of Israel."
2 Kings 3-9 ESV

In 2 Kings 21, we find out that in addition to leading the people away from God, he also had an extremely violent and bloody reign. We learn more about Manasseh from 2 Chronicles 33. We find out that Manasseh is eventually dragged off to Babylon with a hook in his nose. He gets stuck between a rock and a hard place and calls out to God in sincere repentance. God listens to him and has mercy on him bringing Manasseh back to Jerusalem.

When Manasseh returned to Jerusalem, he tried to undo all the evil he had done. But the effects of his sin were catastrophic. The people never did truly come back to God after being led astray. God showed grace to Manasseh, but there were still consequences to the years he spent leading others astray. We can learn a lot from this story.

Your sin doesn't just affect you, but it affects everyone around you. Your choices have consequences, and how you live your life matters! Manasseh led an entire nation away from God. The way you live your day to day life is significant because you will either drive people towards God like Hezekiah or away from God like Manasseh. Which king's example will you follow? Better yet, we should follow the example of King Jesus and lead others to Him. This was the strategy of the apostle Paul.

Follow Me as I Follow Christ

"'I have the right to do anything,' you say—but not everything is beneficial. 'I have the right to do anything'—but not everything is constructive. No one should seek their own good, but the good of others.

Eat anything sold in the meat market without raising questions of conscience, for, 'The earth is the Lord's, and everything in it.'

If an unbeliever invites you to a meal and you want to go, eat whatever is put before you without raising questions of conscience. But if someone says to you, 'This has been offered in sacrifice,' then do not eat it, both for the sake of the one who told you and for the sake of conscience. I am referring to the other person's conscience, not yours. For why is my freedom being judged by another's conscience? If I take part in the meal with thankfulness, why am I denounced because of something I thank God for?

So whether you eat or drink or whatever you do, do it all for the glory of God. Do not cause anyone to stumble, whether Jews, Greeks or the church of God— even as I try to please

everyone in every way. For I am not seeking my own good
but the good of many, so that they may be saved."
1 Corinthians 10:23-33 NIV

In these verses, the apostle Paul is addressing how we should handle the freedom that we have in the Christian life. Paul is making the argument that even though he has this freedom, he is always aware that he is either leading people towards God or pulling them away from Him. He concludes that we shouldn't cause anyone to stumble in their faith. We must continuously be aware of how our actions affect the people around us. It is by living in this way that Paul can confidently say what he does in this next verse,

"Follow my example, as I follow the example of Christ."
1 Corinthians 11:1 NIV

Wow, what a challenge! Paul is saying if you want to follow the example of Christ, follow me because I am following His example. That is a phrase someone with a different spirit would say. If you can't join Paul in saying this yet, don't worry, Rome wasn't built in a day. I'm not there either; don't be discouraged! Don't give up just because you aren't there yet. Keep going. The path to different is what will enable us to lead others to follow the example of Christ.

Real Friends Bring Their Friends to Jesus

The kind of friend you are and who your friends are is essential. Don't underestimate the power of your circle. I can make a good guess about if you are on the path to different based on who you spend the most time around. There is a paralytic man in the Bible who had an outstanding group of friends. This man's four friends went above and beyond to bring him to Jesus. This story is unique, but the principle is not. We must do whatever it takes to get the people we care about in our lives to Jesus! In Mark 2:1-5, we read:

> *"And when he returned to Capernaum after some days,*
> *it was reported that he was at home. And many were*
> *gathered together, so that there was no more room, not*
> *even at the door. And he was preaching the word to them.*
> *And they came, bringing to him a paralytic carried by*
> *four men. And when they could not get near him because*
> *of the crowd, they removed the roof above him, and when*
> *they had made an opening, they let down the bed on*
> *which the paralytic lay. And when Jesus saw their faith,*
> *he said to the paralytic, 'Son, your sins are forgiven.'"*
> Mark 2:1-5 ESV

These four men were great friends. They brought their friend to Jesus because they knew that Jesus was the only one who could heal their friend. Listen, Jesus is the only one who can heal the people you care about as well. To be a good friend, you must follow the example of these four men—what an inspiring story!

We need to be continually evaluating our friendships and asking ourselves if we are bringing our friends closer to Jesus. On the flip side, you need to ask yourself if your friends are bringing you closer to Jesus too. If not, you need to get friends that will pull you closer to Him because real friends bring their friends to Jesus.

Discussion

1. Where are the areas of influence that you have in your life?

2. What are your thoughts on the story of Hezekiah and Manasseh?

3. Are there any areas in your life where you are causing others to stumble in their faith?

4. How are you going to lead others closer to Christ going forward?

5. Are you a friend that leads your friends to Jesus?

6. Do your friends pull you closer to Jesus?

CHAPTER 10

HAVING A DIFFERENT SPIRIT IS WORTH IT

*"But since my servant Caleb has a different spirit and
has remained loyal to me, I will bring him into the land
where he has gone, and his descendants will inherit it."*
Numbers 14:24 CSB

*"No eye has seen, no ear has heard, and no mind has
imagined what God has prepared for those who love him."*
1 Corinthians 2:9 NLT

At some point along this journey on the path to different, you are
going to ask yourself: is this worth it? You may even be asking
yourself that question at this very moment. I pray that this chapter
resolves that question for you.

Nothing motivates me more than being around veteran
Christians—people who have spent forty, fifty, maybe even sixty
years as faithful followers of Jesus. Something that I've noticed is that
none of these people regret their years of devotion to the Lord. They

are filled with passion, and they love their Savior. Caleb was one of these people. He followed the Lord faithfully his entire life. Check out this passage from Joshua 14:

> *"Now then, just as the Lord promised, he has kept me alive for forty-five years since the time he said this to Moses, while Israel moved about in the wilderness. So here I am today, eighty-five years old! I am still as strong today as the day Moses sent me out; I'm just as vigorous to go out to battle now as I was then. Now give me this hill country that the Lord promised me that day. You yourself heard then that the Anakites were there and their cities were large and fortified, but, the Lord helping me, I will drive them out just as he said."*
> Joshua 14:10-12 NIV

At 85 years old, his faith was still as strong as ever. Caleb was able to enter the Promised Land because he had a different spirit, and he stayed loyal to God. Imagine Caleb sitting across from you, and you are talking with him. Pretty cool right? He is telling you the story about spying the land out and about how the people reacted. He tells you he thought he was going to be stoned by his own people. Then, you ask him, "Was it worth it?"

What do you think he would say? I believe, with all my heart, that he would say "Absolutely, it was worth it." He would have never gotten to go to the Promised Land if he listened to everyone else.

The decision to follow Jesus and live for Him is the most significant decision of your entire life. It is a costly decision, and you may lose some friends. But you won't regret it. When you are at the end of your life, you will realize that living to make a difference is infinitely better than living to fit in. You will find that the path to different is not the easy path, but you will find that it's worth it. You will have lived out your purpose in life, which is to glorify God in all that you do, and you will leave your impact on this world. Whatever you do, don't choose the other path. The other spies took this path, which is the same one that many others are on. This path is tempting because it is so well-trodden. But Jesus tells us in the gospel of Mathew:

> *"Enter by the narrow gate. For the gate is wide and the way is easy that leads to destruction, and those who enter by it are many. For the gate is narrow and the way is hard that leads to life, and those who find it are few."*
> Mathew 7:13-14 ESV

The path that you choose is in your hands. I can't make that decision for you. The path to different will enable you to live a life of purpose and impact, but most importantly, it will lead you to Jesus.

A Trip to The Future

Would you like to take a trip to the future? Well, I don't have a time machine, but Revelation 5 gives us a glimpse into what is in store for those who travel on the path to different. If you are on the fence with all of this, check out these verses:

> *"Then I looked, and I heard around the throne and the living creatures and the elders the voice of many angels, numbering myriads of myriads and thousands of thousands, saying with a loud voice, 'Worthy is the Lamb who was slain, to receive power and wealth and wisdom and might and honor and glory and blessing!'"*
> Revelation 5:11-12 ESV

What Will Heaven Be Like?

When I say "heaven," what do you think of? Do you think of sitting on a cloud playing the harp and singing Kumbaya forever? To be honest, that would probably get old quick. That idea of heaven is very boring but sadly very common. Luckily, that is not the heaven that we read about in the Bible. We don't know on this side of eternity exactly what heaven will be like, but what we do know should make us want to go there!

You Will Be You in Heaven (But Better)

Contrary to what many believe, you don't get wings when you get to heaven. You won't suddenly become an angel. You will still be human. You will still be you. This is not meant to be disrespectful in any way, and if this is something you've always believed, don't be discouraged. The fact we don't become angels when we die is good news. When Satan (a former angel) fell, he brought down a third of the other angels with him. However, when the angels fell, God didn't choose to save them like He chose to save us. Jesus never went to the cross to die for angels, but human beings made in the image of God. A country gospel song written by Gordon Jensen captures this truth beautifully. Here are the lyrics:

> "Angels never knew the joy that is mine,
> For the blood has never washed their sins away;
> Though they sing in heaven, there will come a time
> When silently they'll listen to me sing 'Amazing Grace.'
>
> It's a song holy angels cannot sing,
> Amazing Grace, how sweet the sound!
> It's a song holy angels cannot sing,
> I once was lost, but now I'm found!

Holy is the LORD, the angels sing,
All around the throne of GOD continually;
For me to join their song will be a natural thing,
But they just won't know the words to 'Love Lifted Me.'"[1]

You will still have your body in heaven, but it will be a glorified body. Your new body will be much better. Philippians 3:20-21 says:

"But our citizenship is in heaven, and from it we await a Savior, the Lord Jesus Christ, who will transform our lowly body to be like his glorious body, by the power that enables him even to subject all things to himself."
Philippians 3:20-21 ESV

Just imagine the implications of this for a moment. People who spent their whole lives in wheelchairs will be able to run in heaven. The blind will see. The deaf will hear. You won't have healthcare in heaven because you will never need a doctor. You will never feel the aches and pains that you feel in this life again. You will never get tired. It is going to be incredible!

You Will Be Busy

"No longer will there be any curse. The throne of God and of the Lamb will be in the city, and his servants will serve him."
Revelation 22:3 NIV

If the idea of sitting on a cloud forever bores you like it does me, you will love heaven. In heaven, God will have work for you to do. Your work in heaven won't be like work right now. It won't be a burden, and it won't make you tired and weary.

In Genesis, God put Adam to work in the garden. It was only after the fall that this work became difficult. Genesis 3:19 says,

*"By the sweat of your brow you will eat your food until
you return to the ground, since from it you were taken;
for dust you are and to dust you will return."*
Genesis 3:19 NIV

We are not able to work our hardest on this side of eternity without fatigue. In heaven, you will experience work as God intended it, and it will be good. It will be a blessing and not a burden. It will be a privilege and not a problem. You will be able to serve Jesus with unlimited energy. The Bible doesn't tell us precisely what the work is that we will do, but you can rest assured that you won't be bored!

You Will Never Suffer Again (In Heaven)

*"He will wipe away every tear from their eyes, and death
shall be no more, neither shall there be mourning, nor crying,
nor pain anymore, for the former things have passed away."*
Revelation 21:14 ESV

If God is all good and all-powerful, then why doesn't He do anything about all the evil that exists in the world? This is one of the toughest questions in the Christian faith, and I'm not going to pretend like I have the answers. But scripture gives us the assurance that one day there won't be any more evil and that God will do something. He will wipe away the tears from your eyes. There will be no more death. There will be no more mourning. There will be no more pain. Do you know how the Bible describes our suffering on earth?

*"Therefore we do not lose heart. Though outwardly we are
wasting away, yet inwardly we are being renewed day by
day. For our light and momentary troubles are achieving for
us an eternal glory that far outweighs them all. So we fix*

*our eyes not on what is seen, but on what is unseen, since
what is seen is temporary, but what is unseen is eternal."*
2 Corinthians 4:16-18 NIV

Don't lose heart; all the suffering in your life is a light and momentary affliction. It won't be like this forever. Your suffering is not in vain, and it is preparing for you an eternal weight of glory. This is good news that is meant to comfort us. We can look forward to heaven with great anticipation knowing that one day the same God that redeemed us will also restore us.

You Will Have Joy

*"You make known to me the path of life;
you will fill me with joy in your presence,
with eternal pleasures at your right hand."*
Psalm 16:11 NIV

God is the source of all joy, and in His presence, we will experience this wonderful feeling in its fullness. True joy comes from being in the presence of God. All the joy you've experienced in this life is just a shadow of what is to come. We will see God face to face. Have you thought about the joy of that moment? I like what Wayne Grudem says about this in his book *Systematic Theology*:

*"When John speaks of the blessings of the heavenly city, the
culmination of those blessings comes in the short statement,
'they shall see his face' (Rev. 22:4). When we look into
the face of our Lord and he looks back at us with infinite
love, we will see him in the fulfillment of everything
that we know to be good and right and desirable in the
universe. In the face of God, we will see the fulfillment
of all the longing we have ever had to know perfect love,*

peace, and joy, and to know truth and justice, holiness and
wisdom, goodness and power, and glory and beauty."[2]

Final Thoughts on Heaven

There is no way to describe heaven and do it justice. It will be everything you could ever dream of and so much more. Heaven will be perfect. Furthermore, we will get there not because of anything that we do but because of what Jesus has done. Having a different spirit like Caleb is not what gets you to heaven, but if you are heading there, you will have a different spirit. Caleb entered the Promised Land, and by God's grace, we will enter heaven. The path to different is more than worth it. Stick close to it and focus on Jesus along the way. At the end of your life, when you look back, you will have fulfilled your purpose of glorifying God, and you will have made an impact that will last for generations to come.

Discussion

1. Have you ever questioned if following Jesus is worth it?

2. What is your response to reading Revelation 5:11-12?

3. What did you think heaven was like before reading this chapter?

4. What do you think heaven will be like after reading this chapter?

5. Do you agree that the path to different is worth it?

CHAPTER 11

A DIFFERENT SPIRIT LEAVES A LEGACY THAT INSPIRES OTHERS

"The Israelites cried out to the Lord. So the Lord raised up Othniel son of Kenaz, Caleb's youngest brother, as a deliverer to save the Israelites."
Judges 3:9 CSB

"The greatest legacy one can pass on to one's children and grandchildren is not money or other material things accumulated in one's life, but rather a legacy of character and faith,"
Billy Graham

As a young person getting started in ministry, Billy Graham became one of my spiritual heroes. The thing that inspired me most about Billy Graham was not that he preached to millions. What inspired me was the humility and faithfulness that he demonstrated decade after decade in ministry. He had such a clear mission in life. You may not know this, but during the height of his ministry, Billy Graham was asked to run for president of the United States.

He decided not to run because he said that wasn't his mission. His mission was to preach the gospel of Jesus Christ. I hope and pray that I will possess the same laser-like focus in my own life and ministry.

Billy Graham passed away on February 21ˢᵗ, 2018. The legacy that he left behind is nothing short of incredible. Most of his children and grandchildren followed in his footsteps by going into the ministry. He was a hero of the faith. Caleb was a hero of the faith back in his day. Just like Billy Graham, he had family members that followed in his footsteps.

Othniel: The First Judge

Othniel was Caleb's nephew. Imagine growing up with Caleb as a family member. He probably told Othniel stories about the time he spent in Egypt and about how God rescued him out of slavery. He more than likely told him about how God parted the Red Sea and how God provided for him and the other Israelites during their forty years of wandering around in the wilderness. How inspiring would it be to hear from Caleb's mouth the story of how God allowed him into the Promised Land for having a different spirit? I'm sure he was a huge role model for Othniel. He took after Caleb in many ways. Check out what the Bible says about him in Judges 3:

> *"The Israelites did what was evil in the Lord's sight;*
> *they forgot the Lord their God and worshiped the Baals*
> *and the Asherahs. The Lord's anger burned against Israel,*
> *and he sold them to King Cushan-rishathaim of*
> *Aram-naharaim, and the Israelites served him eight*
> *years. The Israelites cried out to the Lord. So the Lord*
> *raised up Othniel son of Kenaz, Caleb's youngest*
> *brother, as a deliverer to save the Israelites."*
> Judges 3:7-9 CSB

When Israel was in trouble, God used Othniel to save them. Othniel became the first judge of Israel. The judges in the Bible were not judges like we think of today. They were people that God raised to deliver Israel. They would save Israel if they found themselves in trouble. There were some good judges, and there were some very bad judges. Othniel was one of the good ones.

Othniel Had a Different Spirit Like Caleb

> *"The Spirit of the Lord came on him, and he judged*
> *Israel. Othniel went out to battle, and the Lord*
> *handed over King Cushan-rishathaim of Aram*
> *to him, so that Othniel overpowered him."*
> Judges 3:10 CSB

Othniel, like Caleb, was filled with a different spirit. This verse says that Othniel was filled with the Holy Spirit while he was a judge. It is tough to read about his story without seeing the influence of Caleb on his life. He was courageous, strong, and faithful, just like his uncle. How will the people who follow in your footsteps look? You may not be proud of your steps right now. That's okay. Make new footsteps on the path to different. Your past failures don't determine your future effectiveness for God. He uses imperfect people to accomplish His perfect will.

Doubting Thomas

> *"Now Thomas, one of the twelve, called the Twin, was*
> *not with them when Jesus came. So the other disciples*
> *told him, 'We have seen the Lord.' But he said to them,*
> *'Unless I see in his hands the mark of the nails, and*
> *place my finger into the mark of the nails, and*

place my hand into his side, I will never believe.'"
John 20:24-25 esv

When you think of Thomas in the Bible, you probably think of his nickname, "doubting Thomas." Do you think Thomas meant for his legacy to be that he was a doubter? I don't think so. I don't believe he was thinking about his legacy at all. That's an issue with most people. Not many are concerned with their legacy. They are just living life moment to moment, not thinking long term about how people will remember them or what sort of legacy they will leave behind. Having a different spirit will require you to have a different mindset.

A Man After God's Own Heart

David was a man who knew how to leave a legacy. You have probably heard the story of David defeating the giant, Goliath. Perhaps, you have heard him called "a man after God's own heart." He spent a lifetime building his legacy. Of course, David made some huge mistakes in his life. He committed adultery and had someone murdered to cover it up. But overall, David is remembered very positively. He knew the legacy he wanted to leave, and before David passed away, he gave Solomon some last words of encouragement.

> *"When David's time to die drew near, he commanded Solomon his son, saying, 'I am about to go the way of all the earth. Be strong, and show yourself a man, and keep the charge of the Lord your God, walking in his ways and keeping his statutes, his commandments, his rules, and his testimonies, as it is written in the Law of Moses, that you may prosper in all that you do and wherever you turn, that the Lord may establish his word that he spoke concerning me, saying, 'If your sons pay close attention to their way, to walk before me in faithfulness with all their heart and with all*

their soul, you shall not lack a man on the throne of Israel.'"
1 Kings 2:1-4 ESV

What wise words for us all. What would your last moments of encouragement be? I don't believe in reinventing the wheel so mine would be remarkably similar to David's. May we all learn from his example of leaving a legacy.

A Legacy That Outlives You

"By faith Abel offered to God a more acceptable sacrifice than Cain, through which he was commended as righteous, God commending him by accepting his gifts. And through his faith, though he died, he still speaks."
Hebrews 11:4

Abel was the first person to be murdered in history. His brother Cain killed him. However, the Bible says that even though Abel is dead, his legacy of faith lives on. He still speaks to us today. The path to different will enable your legacy to live on after you are gone. You will still speak to and inspire the generations to come. Check out Psalm 145:4:

"One generation shall commend your works to another, and shall declare your mighty acts."
Psalm 145:4 ESV

Start thinking now rather than later about what kind of legacy you want to leave. Will it be a legacy that inspires others? Will it be a legacy of character and faith? The path to different will allow you to leave a legacy that outlives you. It will be a legacy that above all else, points others to Jesus. Caleb left a legacy that has inspired me, and I hope it inspires you as well.

Your Dash

At the end of your life, on your tombstone there will be two dates. Your birthdate and your death date. But that's not really what matters. What matters is the little dash that will be between those two dates. That dash is your life. Your legacy will be determined by how you spend your dash. Caleb spent his dash well. How will you spend yours? Think about this amazing poem by Linda Ellis:

The Dash Poem
"I read of a man who stood to speak at the
funeral of a friend. He referred to the dates on the
tombstone from the beginning… to the end.
He noted that first came the date of birth and spoke of
the following date with tears, but he said what mattered
most of all was the dash between those years.
For that dash represents all the time they spent
alive on earth and now only those who loved
them know what that little line is worth.
For it matters not, how much we own, the cars…
the house… the cash. What matters is how we
live and love and how we spend our dash.
So think about this long and hard; are there things
you'd like to change? For you never know how
much time is left that still can be rearranged.
To be less quick to anger and show appreciation more and
love the people in our lives like we've never loved before.
If we treat each other with respect and more
often wear a smile… remembering that this
special dash might only last a little while.
So when your eulogy is being read, with your life's
actions to rehash, would you be proud of the things
they say about how you lived your dash?"

Discussion

1. Have you ever thought about what people will remember you for?

2. Define legacy in your own words

3. Who has left a legacy that has inspired you?

4. After reading this chapter, what do you want your legacy to be?

CHAPTER 12

CONCLUSION

We have been conditioned our entire lives for one path: conformity. We learn from a very young age a desire to fit in. I look back and laugh at all the fads I fell into growing up in a pitiful attempt to fit in with my peers. I remember being in kindergarten during the nineties and tying my jacket around my waist because that was the cool thing to do. I remember scuffing up my jeans so that they would have holes in the knees. I remember in 5th grade having to have a particular fleece jacket that everyone else wore, and I had to have. I remember getting a pair of boat shoes in middle school just because everyone else wore them. If you were born in the early nineties like me, you probably just had a tiny wave of nostalgia sweep over you.

I could go on and on, but the point is that we all have a desire to fit in and to be accepted. Each of us has a table that we want to be invited to. On the flip side, most people also have a desire to make a difference. At some point in life, you must decide which desire you want to follow, which path you choose. You can't have it both ways. No one can serve two masters (Mathew 6:24). I've written this book to try to steer you down the path that can fulfill your desire to make a difference while also fulfilling God's purpose in you, which is to glorify Him. It is God's will for you to live of purpose and impact. He has you here for a reason, and you aren't just taking up space. You have a part in the amazing story that God is telling the world. If you find that hard to believe, check out Ephesians 3:20 which says:

"Now to him who is able to do immeasurably
more than all we ask or imagine, according
to his power that is at work within us"
Ephesians 3:20 NIV

You may feel inadequate or unqualified, but you have no idea the difference that you can make in this world when God works through you. When I was called into ministry, I thought there is no way God was calling me to do this. I ran from my calling for a while because I believed it was a mistake; He couldn't be that desperate! Eventually, I gave in and pursued God's calling. Since finally surrendering to the ministry, I've found this verse to be true in my life. What I've come to realize is that all God needed me to be was available. He can do immeasurably more than you could ever ask or even imagine. It is His power that is at work within you, and it doesn't matter your age, your income, what family you came from, or what happened in your past. God can use you. He wants to use you, just let Him, and then, sit back and be amazed.

Caleb had a different spirit, but he was human like us. He gives us an excellent example of someone who chose the path to different, but he wasn't perfect. We've taken away some valuable principles from his life, but the ultimate example we have is Jesus. However, Jesus being our example isn't good news. We can never live up to His example. The good news is that Jesus is more than just our example.

He is our substitute. He loved you enough to die for you on a cross. He rose to life again so that you and I could also be raised to a new life with Him. He offers us abundant life in Him, according to John 10:10. Why would you want to settle for anything less?

The abundant life that God offers will require you to be entirely dependent on God and not yourself. You cannot make a difference for the kingdom of God by just trying really hard. All your efforts will be in vain unless it is God who is working through you.

> *"I am the vine; you are the branches. If you remain in me and I in you, you will bear much fruit; apart from me you can do nothing."*
> John 15:5 NIV

If you want to live a life of purpose and impact, walk with Jesus. Spend time with Him in prayer, study His Word, and get involved in church. God will change you into the difference maker He has called you to be and you will play your role in the Great Commission (Matthew 28:18-20). I prayerfully hope that God has used this book in your life for His glory and that He blesses you on your journey down the path to different.

ACKNOWLEDGMENTS

Taylor, I could never have finished this book without your love and support. I love you so much, and I thank the Lord for you each and every day. Mom and Dad, thank you for always encouraging me and believing in me. Emily, you are the best little sister in the entire world, and I am so proud of you. To the rest of my family, I love and appreciate all of you.

I want to thank the many mentors in my life that have made this book possible. I have been extremely blessed with the people God has placed in my life.

To Dr. Billy Joy, I am so grateful for your leadership and influence in my life. Thank you for supporting me in my call to ministry. I love you and your family like my own.

To TJ Joy, thank you for investing in me. I appreciate your friendship more than you will ever know.

To Hank Atchison, God used you at a crucial time in my life when you were my youth pastor, and I look up to you so much.

To Drew Dockery, Todd Bridges, and Andy Pugh thank you for all that you taught me about life and ministry during college. The Lord used all of you to mold and encourage me. Drew, you taught me so much about being in ministry and discipleship. Todd, you showed me how to have a passion for missions. Mr. Andy, you and Mrs. Angie demonstrated what true hospitality looks like to me and so many others.

To Brian Jennings, Chris Page, and Joseph Gibbons thank you for all that you taught me as an intern starting in ministry. I use the lessons you taught me every day.

To Pastor Johnny, I am forever grateful for your influence on my life. Thank you for taking the time to invest in me and encourage me. You are one of the busiest pastors in the world, but somehow you still find time to take interns to lunch. It has been an honor to learn so much about ministry and leadership from you.

To Brother Ken and the rest of Centreville Baptist Church, thank you for giving me my first opportunity in ministry. I love you guys. Brother Ken, it has been a joy and a privilege to serve under your leadership. Your faithfulness in ministry is an inspiration to me.

To the faculty and staff at Leavell College, I am indebted to you for your role in preparing me for the ministry. Choosing this institution for my education has been one of the best decisions of my life.

To all my students, I love every one of you. This book flows out of that love for you. I hope it serves you well and is a valuable resource for you and your walk with Christ.

To my friends who are more like family, you know who you are. I thank God every day for surrounding me with such amazing people. I love all of you.

Finally, I want to give a huge thank you to Ben Birdsong for editing this book. You are the best!

RECOMMENDED READING

C.S. Lewis, *The Problem of Pain* (HarperOne)

Francis Chan, *The Forgotten God* (David C. Cook)

Francis Chan, *Crazy Love* (David C. Cook)

Jared C. Wilson, *Supernatural Power for Everyday People* (Thomas Nelson)

Jared C. Wilson, *Gospel Wakefulness* (Crossway)

David Platt, *Radical* (Multnomah)

Taylor Morton, *It's Only Pain: But It's Real and It Hurts* (The Core Media Group, Inc.)

Brent Crowe, *Sacred Intent: Maximize the Moments of Your Life* (Worthy Books)

Johnny Hunt, *Demolishing Strongholds: Finding Victory Over the Struggles That Hold You Back* (Harvest House Publishers)

Matt Brown, *Truth Plus Love: The Jesus Way to Influence* (Zondervan)

Shane Pruitt, *9 Common Lies Christians Believe: And Why God's Truth Is Infinitely Better* (Multnomah)

Robby Gallaty, *Growing Up: How to Be a Disciple Who Makes Disciples* (B&H Books)

Billy Graham, *The Holy Spirit* (Thomas Nelson)

J.D. Greear, *Jesus Continued: Why the Spirit Inside You Is Better Than Jesus Beside You* (Zondervan)

Dean Inserra, *The Unsaved Christian* (Moody Publishers)

Matt Chandler, *Recovering Redemption: A Gospel Saturated Perspective on How to Change* (B&H Books)

Louie Giglio, *Not Forsaken: Finding Freedom as Sons & Daughters of a Perfect Father* (B&H Books)

Bob Goff, *Love Does: Discover a Secretly Incredible Life in an Ordinary World* (Thomas Nelson)

Levi Lusko, *I Declare War: Four Keys to Winning the Battle with Yourself* (Thomas Nelson)

Greg Laurie, *Jesus Revolution: How God Transformed an Unlikely Generation and How He Can Do It Again Today* (Baker Books)

Kevin DeYoung, *Just Do Something: A Liberating Approach to Finding God's Will* (Moody Publishers)

Dustin Willis & Aaron Coe, *Life on Mission: Joining the Everyday Mission of God* (Moody Publishers)

Alvin Reid, *Sharing Jesus without Freaking Out: Evangelism the Way You Were Born to Do It* (B&H Academic)

NOTES

Chapter 1

1. Warren, Rick, *The Purpose Driven Life* (Grand Rapids: Zondervan, 2002), 29.

Chapter 2

1. *Online Etymology Dictionary*, https://www.etymonline.com/word/encourage (accessed July 12, 2019).
2. Crabb, Larry and Dan B. Allender, *Encouragement: The Unexpected Power of Building Others Up* (Grand Rapids: Zondervan, 2013), 88.

Chapter 3

1. Acuff, Jon, *Start: Punch Fear in the Face, Escape Average, and Do Work that Matters* (Nashville: Ramsey Press, 2013), 89.
2. Terry, Lindsay, "The Story Behind the Song: 'Because He Lives,'" *The St. Augustine Record*, https://www.staugustine.com/article/20150129/LIFESTYLE/301299969 (accessed July 12, 2019).

3. Gaither, Bill and Gloria Gaither, "Because He Lives," Gaither Copyright Management, 1971.

Chapter 4

1. Warren, Rick, Twitter Post, November 14, 2013, 7:00 p.m., https://twitter.com/rickwarren/status/40118292098 4899584?lang=en

2. Pruitt, Shane, *9 Common Lies Christians Believe: And Why God's Truth Is Indefinitely Better* (Colorado Springs: Multnomah, 2019), 141.

3. Laurie, Greg, *Tell Someone: You Can Share the Good News* (Nashville: B&H Books, 2016), 14.

Chapter 5

1. IVP New Testament Commentary, *Bible Gateway*, https://www.biblegateway.com/resources/commentaries/IVP-NT/John/Jesus-Introduces-Major-Themes (accessed July 15, 2019).

2. Challies, Tim, "Do Not Be Surprised if the World Hates You," *Challies.com*, https://www.challies.com/articles/do-not-be-surprised-if-the-world-hates-you/ (accessed July 15, 2019).

3. Tertullian, *Apologeticus,* 50.

4. Morrison, J. G. "Wesley's Expectation of Persecution," *The Character Journal*, https://www.characterjournal.com/wesleys-expectation-of-persecution/ (accessed July 15, 2019).

Chapter 6

1. Kelley, Michael, "3 Things that Keep Christians from Living with a Sense of Urgency," *For the Church*, https://

ftc.co/resource-library/blog-entries/3-things-that-keep-christians-from-living-with-a-sense-of-urgency (accessed July 16, 2019).

2. Buhler, Rich, "Alabama Coach Paul 'Bear' Bryant Carried a Prayer in His Wallet- Truth!," *TruthorFiction.com*, https://www.truthorfiction.com/alabama-coach-paul-bear-bryant-carried-a-prayer-in-his-wallet/ (accessed July 16, 2019).

Chapter 7

1. Grudem, Wayne, *Systematic Theology: An Introduction to Biblical Doctrine* (Grand Rapids: Zondervan, 1994), 634.

Chapter 8

1. Inserra, Dean, *The Unsaved Christian: Reaching Cultural Christianity with the Gospel* (Chicago: Moody, 2019), 16-17.

Chapter 9

1. "Meet Hezekiah: Successful King of Judah, " *Learn Religions*, https://www.learnreligions.com/hezekiah-successful-king-of-judah-4089408 (accessed July 17, 2019).

Chapter 10

1. Jensen, Gordon, "A Song Holy Angels Cannot Sing," https://www.classic-country-song-lyrics.com/asongholyangelscannotsinglyricschords.html (accessed July 17, 2019).

2. Grudem, Wayne, *Systematic Theology: An Introduction to Biblical Doctrine* (Grand Rapids: Zondervan, 1994), 1164.

Chapter 11

1. Billy Graham Celebrates 93rd Birthday Following Release of 30th Book, 'Nearing Home,' *BillyGramam.Org*,https://billygraham.org/press-release/billy-graham-celebrates-93rd-birthday-following-release-of-30th-book-nearing-home/ (accessed August 14, 2019).

2. David Frost, President Billy Graham? "How the evangelist came close to running for the Oval Office," *Christianity Today*, https://www.christiantoday.com/article/president-billy-graham-how-the-evangelist-came-close-to-running-for-the-oval-office/127150.htm (accessed August 14, 2019).

3. Linda Frost, "The Dash," *TheDashPoem.com,* https://thedashpoem.com/ (accessed August 14, 2019).

I'd Love to Hear from You

If you have found this book has helped you in any way, or if you have any questions, I would love to connect with you!

Facebook – Lonnie Free
Instagram/Twitter – @Lonnie_Free
Email – freelonnie1@gmail.com

52550970R00080

Made in the USA
Lexington, KY
16 September 2019